Sports Illustrated

The College Basketball Book

THE BALL Rio Grande's Clarence (Bevo) Francis used to score 113 points in a game in 1954.

1968 | CENTERS' STAGE was the
Astrodome, and the stars were the focus
as Elvin Hayes (right) and Lew Alcindor
tipped off a legendary showdown.

Photograph by NEIL LEIFER

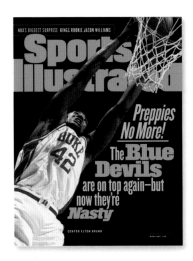

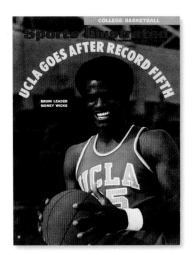

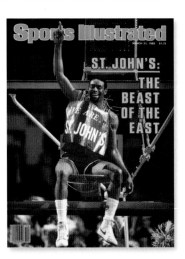

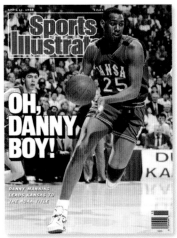

The College Basketball Book

GREG KELLY
Editor

STEVEN HOFFMAN
Designer

CRISTINA SCALET *Photo Editor*   DON DELLIQUANTI *Assistant Photo Editor*

KEVIN KERR *Copy Editor*   DAVID SABINO *Associate Editor*

JOSH DENKIN *Associate Designer*   MATT GAGNE, KELVIN BIAS *Reporters*

STEFANIE KAUFMAN *Project Manager*

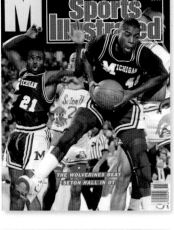

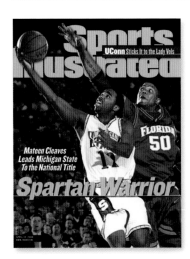

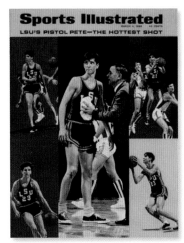

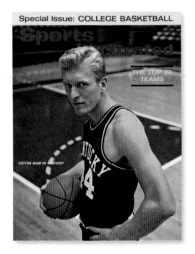

Sports Illustrated
Contents

BILL WALTON
The Big Redhead, UCLA
1971
Photograph by GEORGE LONG

1964 | THE MAN in the mirror was Kentucky coach Adolph Rupp as the Baron addressed the Wildcats before a game against Mississippi. | *Photograph by* RICH CLARKSON

2001 | BASKETBALL TURNED into dominoes in Duke's title-game victory as the Blue Devils' Shane Battier and Arizona's Eugene Edgerson battled on the boards and sent bodies flying. | *Photograph by* JOHN W. MCDONOUGH

THE PLAY IS THE THING

BY ALEXANDER WOLFF

A LANKY YOUNG MAN WITH A BALL: IT MAKES FOR an iconic tableau, a reminder of how basketball and a child get acquainted. But look across at the sequence of pictures of Hank Luisetti, the Stanford star from the 1930s. The relationship is farther along now. There's a whiff of the collegiate here—of self-discovery and experimentation. Luisetti is noodling with his game. (Ever hear a baseball or football player refer to "my game?") All that's missing from these images are the trappings of a laboratory, as well as (and here's the point) some instructor in a lab coat. It would be easy to conclude from much of the text that wraps around the pictures in this book—indeed, from the prevailing cultural narrative of college basketball, set largely by coaches-turned-TV-pundits who puff up their erstwhile brothers of the lodge—that the coach made the game what it is and that it abidingly belongs to him. Consider, instead, the gym as a lab, the place where college kids literally invented their version of the sport, one innovation at a time.

STYLE POINTS have long been a feature of the game, as Stanford's Luisetti demonstrated with a behind-the-back dribble for LIFE's cameras in 1938.

Behold their firsts: Luisetti using one hand to shoot, and revolutionaries like Wyoming's Kenny Sailors leaving their feet to do so; Seton Hall's Bob Davies wowing crowds with his dribbling, and Holy Cross's Bob Cousy stunning them with his passing; Oklahoma A&M's Bob (Foothills) Kurland placing the ball directly in the basket, in a fashion that one flummoxed reporter called "a duffer shot." Soon successors matched those pioneers' inventiveness with an exuberance that we came to recognize as the very essence of the game. That joy was there in 5' 9" Calvin Murphy, a champion baton-twirler who brought the same showmanship to Niagara's backcourt. It was there in Kenny Dennard, who introduced his teammates on Duke's 1978 Final Four team to elaborate high fives inspired by *The Rocky Horror Picture Show*. And it was there in every one of the rim-rattling slams—no "duffer shots" they—thrown down during the 1983 national semifinal in which the frat brothers of Houston's Phi Slamma Jamma and Louisville's Doctors of Dunk showered one another with verbal bouquets while running up and down the floor, sending reserves scrambling from benches to catch replays on the monitors along press row. You know that cloying coinage "student-athlete?" Neither word comes close to capturing any of this. College basketball is populated by players—kids at play.

If you doubt it, cock your ear toward Ali Farokhmanesh (*above*), and damned if you can't hear his primal scream leap off the page as he and ninth-seeded Northern Iowa upset No. 1–seeded Kansas in the second round of the 2010 NCAA tournament. Or turn the next page and behold the boy-king Cozell McQueen, surmounted on his throne after North Carolina State's upset of Houston in the 1983 title game. Or check out the lip-curdling despair in the photo on page 77, which captures Southeast Missouri's Lawrence Wilson in the aftermath of the Indians' loss to North Carolina Central in the 1989 NCAA Division II national championship final. Indeed, the game can pour joy and agony into a single frame, as attested to by the image on the opposite page, from the conclusion of the 2005 Chicago Regional final between victorious Illinois and defeated Arizona.

Played by men and women still in the flush of youth, witnessed by student sections packed with peers, college basketball is surely our most emotional game. Crammed into the middle of the school year, between football season and spring break, it comes to us in concentrate, units of a mere 40 minutes strung together over four compressed months, and capped by a largely meritocratic, endearingly unpredictable three-week tournament to determine a champion. And it's our most exciting game, with its contests decided right at the finish more reliably than any other sport's. Here again the coach's role is overstated: Yes, the surgical, final-seconds play with which Bryce Drew and Valparaiso upset Mississippi in the 1998 NCAAs had been assiduously practiced, and Christian Laettner's turnaround jumper, which sent Duke past Kentucky at the buzzer of the '92 East Regional final, had been more or less drawn up. But so many others weren't: not the full-court rushes of BYU's Danny Ainge in '81 and UCLA's Tyus Edney in '95; not the golden retrieval of Lorenzo Charles, who turned a teammate's air ball into a title-winning dunk for North Carolina State in '83; not Keith Smart's floating championship-clinching jumper from the baseline for Indiana in '87, nor Mario Chalmers's three-point prayer to give Kansas an overtime reprieve and an eventual title in 2008, nor the cold-blooded, title-winning free throws of Joe Quigg for North Carolina in '57 and Rumeal Robinson for Michigan in '89. Again and again these individual, sometimes wholly instinctive acts have vindicated James Naismith's pronunciamento that "Basketball is a game that cannot be coached. It can only be played."

To be a college basketball coach is to learn the truth of the inventor's words cruelly and repeatedly. You're out of timeouts. A pimply freshman holds your team's fate—your livelihood—in his hands. The damned ref won't, despite your entreaties and fulminations (which threaten to unravel the intricate threadwork of your Italian designer suit), make the damned call. In this most entropic of games, things fall apart. The center does not hold . . . the friggin' ball, dammit!

ALI FAROKHMANESH of ninth-seeded Northern Iowa couldn't contain his joy after burying a critical trey in an upset of No. 1–seeded Kansas in the 2010 NCAAs.

Much of the fun of watching college basketball is seeing coaches come to terms with the recurrent realization of their futility. They are the first to tell you how put-upon they are, besieged not just by incompetent referees, but also by the alumni, the press, the admissions office, the Javerts of the NCAA, or some yet-to-be-posted-but-surely-incriminating YouTube video or camera-phone jpeg. Marquette coach and hoops philosophe Al McGuire understood perfectly the great existential uncertainty at the heart of his vocation. To be a college coach, he once said, is to know that "the cheerleader can get pregnant."

Even coaches have a way of reminding us how essentially the game turns back to the players. Listen to the roguish frankness of former Oklahoma coach Billy Tubbs: "Just give us each a budget, a pot of money to spend on players, and there'd be a kind of honor among thieves." Or to UNLV's Jerry Tarkanian, who famously said, "I like transfers. Their cars are already paid for."

The typical undergrad would struggle to match the sophomoric standards of some coaches. LSU's Dale Brown once vowed not to sleep through the duration of an SEC tournament, and phoned sportswriters at all hours lest they doubted his word. Michigan coach Bill Frieder, perpetually and single-mindedly in search of his next great star, once heard another recruiter say, "If Bo Derek's a 10, [schoolboy star Glenn (Doc)] Rivers is at least a nine." To which Frieder replied: "Forget about Rivers. Who's this Bo Derek kid?" Small wonder that coaches sometimes wind up where we expect adolescents: on probation.

The coaches serve a purpose, of course. In the deep pile of their corner office suites, the figures long identified with a single school—the Jim Boeheims and Jim Calhouns, the Mike Krzyzewskis and Tom Izzos—serve as polestars, lending the modern sport, with its roster churn and coachly job-hopping, a useful continuity. Their magisterial predecessors—Phog Allen, Adolph Rupp, John Wooden, Dean Smith—did much to establish the game at a time when spectator sports were seen as little more than baseball, bowl games and the NFL.

Some were just entertaining, like Abe Lemons, who coached at Oklahoma City and Texas and once called the Final Fours of the Wooden era "UCLA bullfights": "You gore the matador all night. In the end, he sticks it in you and the donkeys come on and drag you out."

Gamboling around the tent poles of St. Patrick's Day and April Fool's, the NCAA tournament has a reliable way of encompassing the heedless revelry and Irish fatalism of the former, as well as the whoopee-cushion preposterousness of the latter. The NCAAs and commercial TV began at the same time, in 1939, when the Tall Firs of Oregon won the first title, with one Urgel (Slim) Wintermute anchoring the middle. But the game's great inflection point wouldn't arrive for another 40 years, after the UCLA toreador had finally been vanquished. That's when the Big East was born; when ESPN threw up its first satellite dish; and when Michigan State's Magic Johnson and Indiana State's Larry Bird hooked up in the most-watched NCAA final ever. Since then the cult brothers of Urgel Wintermute—not just Ali Farokhmanesh and Cozell McQueen, but Fennis Dembo and Kevin Pittsnogle, and Wallace (Wah Wah) Jones and (Never Nervous) Pervis Ellison—have carried March Madness to a new standing.

IF A THREAD of proprietorship seems to run through this book, it's because SPORTS ILLUSTRATED grew in parallel with college basketball. You could even say that the two helped make each other.

When SI began in the 1950s as a loss leader for Henry Luce's Time & Life empire, college hoops was a regional sport. It flourished mostly in parochial pockets like New York City, Philadelphia, the Missouri and Ohio river valleys, and the Bay Area, attracting more attention from gamblers than anyone else. As a result, even a phenomenon as large as Wilt Chamberlain remained something of a mystery. "When we played Wilt in '57, he was a god, one of the most famous guys in the country," recalled Tommy Kearns, a member of the North Carolina title team that upset Kansas and the 7' 1" Chamberlain that year. "But we had never really seen him."

THE EMPTINESS of a season's sudden end hit Arizona's Jawann McClellan hard as Illinois celebrated a one-point overtime win that put it in the 2005 Final Four.

SI's romance with the game begins with a man we might call the prophet Jeremiah. Just before the turn of the '60s, writer Jeremiah (Jerry) Tax persuaded SI's editors that a national magazine had a chance to throw a canopy over this far-flung sport. As Tax would pinball from Cal and San Francisco, to Bradley and Cincinnati, to Kansas and Kentucky, and back to the Catholic and public-school redoubts of the urban Northeast, he would carry word of what he had seen to news-starved coaches and local sportswriters, and a thinly chronicled sport gradually came into focus.

Pictures helped too. As you leaf through the images in this book, you may notice a starburst of white in an otherwise pristine image. This is the flash of a strobe light. Think of the basketball photographer as a pastry chef, and the strobe is the finishing tool of his trade, the device used to frost and flash-freeze a moment for later savoring. Firing from the rafters overhead and the lips of tunnels, strobe lights played a huge role in SI's efforts to flog the sport to a broader audience. In advance of a big game the magazine's photographers and their assistants made perilous ascents into catwalks to install them, so subscribers might behold every bead of sweat on a player's limb and every fiber in a cheerleader's sweater.

By the mid-1960s, thanks to SI's weekly exertions, parties to the game had "seen" the landscape of which they were a part. The fans soon followed. In '73, when the title game moved from Saturday afternoon to its current slot in prime time on Monday night, SI began its practice of holding open that week's magazine to accommodate the cover and late-closing pages. Longtime Big Ten commissioner and NCAA tournament committee chair Wayne Duke would credit this decision with helping to vault the Final Four into the top tier of sports events. Eventually even the Oscars fled to another night.

Some of the magazine's most distinctive writers found their muses on the college beat, including Frank Deford, who logged time in Kentucky's locker room as the team waited to take the court in the 1966 NCAA final against Texas Western, and Curry Kirkpatrick, whose New Journalist's voice brought to life rebel spirits like (Pistol) Pete Maravich, Johnny Neumann and Dwight (Bo) Lamar. In the late '70s, back on the collegiate beat after a sojourn covering the NBA, Kirkpatrick explained how he now understood "that at the college level basketball is a happier event, more vibrant, colorful, exciting; that it is better—if not more skillfully—played, better coached and, yes, better officiated; that it is more enthusiastically followed by its fans and more artfully covered by television; that it is esthetically superior, technically more correct, often inspirational; that it is more meaningful than its counterpart. What brought the comparison into sharper focus was that on the rare occasions last spring that I could steal away for a college game, something invari-

ably would happen that was spontaneous, adventuresome. Something would happen that was imaginative, different. Something would happen that was fun. Quite simply, something would happen."

Sometimes what happened had a significance that went beyond the court. During the early '60s, even college coaches who fielded integrated teams still threw a nervous side-glance at the bigots in the booster club, often taking pains to play the proverbial "one black player at home, two on the road and three when you're behind." In its '66 Final Four preview SI noted that "all seven of the Texas Western regulars are Negroes"; after '66, as Al McGuire put it, "We could all stop counting."

But then college basketball has often subverted the established order. In 1944, as his fellow Japanese-Americans filled up internment camps out West, a guard for Utah, Wat Misaka, won over crowds at Madison Square Garden as the Utes won the NCAA title and then beat the NIT champs in a benefit game for the Red Cross. In 1963, three years before Texas Western's title, the call of the NCAA tournament inspired an all-white Mississippi State team to defy a court order from a segregationist judge and sneak out of the state to take on an integrated Loyola of Chicago team *(page 104)*. And thanks to Cheryl Miller, Pat Summitt, and the pioneering women who came before them, Title IX is no longer regarded as something the feds force down reluctant throats, but what lures even male chauvinists to the college hoops trough for a second helping. And while it's impossible to know all the social influences of the game, consider this: When a basketball-obsessed Barack Obama, brother-in-law of an Ivy League player of the year-turned Pac-10 coach, became President in 2008, the two reddest states he flipped to blue—North Carolina and Indiana— were places where college basketball had done much to moot the matter of race.

One night in March 1966, on the eve of college basketball's *Brown* v. *Board of Ed* game between Kentucky and Texas Western, Miners coach Don Haskins thought he had tucked his players into bed at the team's motel in College Park, Md. That's when a clutch of students from the host school, the University of Maryland, showed up in the motel parking lot, carousing and raising a racket. Afraid that they'd wake his players, Haskins invited them to his room and joined them in throwing back beers until dawn.

In that vigil, as much as in what would unspool the following evening, Haskins bore witness to what college basketball is. It is a sit-in. It is a frat party. It is a jubilee that no authority figure has yet figured out how to subdue. It is unbridled youth staging every year a pageant to remind us that we were once young too, and that when you're young, something—anything—can happen. □

COZELL McQUEEN of N.C. State was on top of the world as he celebrated the Wolfpack's last-second upset of Houston in the 1983 NCAA championship game.

The College Bas Book

A Celebration Of the Game

ketball

1995 | FLYING TIGERS (from left) Cedric Henderson, Mingo Johnson, Lorenzen Wright, Chris Garner and Michael Wilson leaped at the chance to star at Memphis. | *Photograph by* LOIS GREENFIELD

2007 | EVEN A long shot of a short shot shows how dominant Ohio State's Greg Oden could be as he unleashed a hook over Georgetown in a Final Four semifinal win. | *Photograph by* BOB ROSATO

2005 | DEE BROWN of Illinois was popping with pride after the Illini went into Carver-Hawkeye Arena and beat Iowa. | *Photograph by* AL TIELEMANS

2011 | ARMORED AND DANGEROUS, UConn's Kemba Walker could barely contain himself after his buzzer beater knocked Pitt out of the Big East tournament. | *Photograph by* RICH KANE

1964 | JEFF MULLINS (44) lost his scoring duel with Cazzie Russell (33) of Michigan, 31–21,
but Duke advanced with a 91–80 win in the Final Four semis. | *Photograph by* HY PESKIN

1895 | SMITH COLLEGE, the birthplace of women's basketball, first competed in 1893, two years after Naismith invented the game. | *Photograph courtesy of the* SMITH COLLEGE ARCHIVES

2002 | CANDICE PHELPS of VCU shows that the women's game is now as in-your-face as the men's, and far gone from its three dribbles and a pass days. | *Photograph by* SCOTT K. BROWN

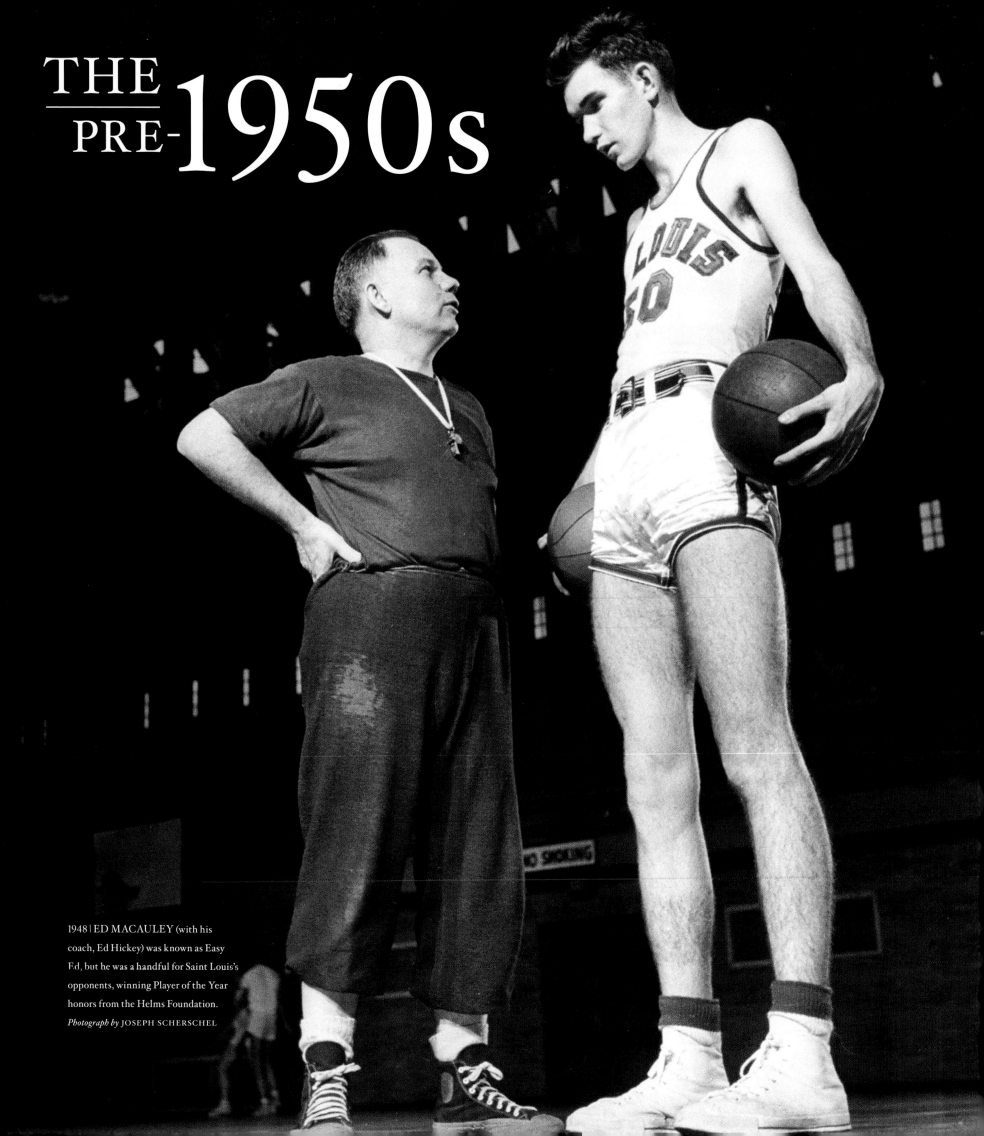

THE PRE-1950s

1948 | ED MACAULEY (with his coach, Ed Hickey) was known as Easy Ed, but he was a handful for Saint Louis's opponents, winning Player of the Year honors from the Helms Foundation.

Photograph by JOSEPH SCHERSCHEL

>> START OF SOMETHING BIG

IN MARCH OF 1939, AS Hitler carved up Czechoslovakia and Mohandas Gandhi began a fast to protest British imperial rule in India, college campuses in the U.S. were obsessed with something slightly less dire: the goldfish-eating craze. And international affairs weren't the only thing being ignored—the first edition of what would become the NCAA tournament also debuted that year, generating little interest and a deficit of $2,531. It was run by the National Association of Basketball Coaches, which blanched at the loss and, with poor financial foresight, turned the tournament over to the NCAA to run.

Many players were too tall to serve with Ike.

New York City's Madison Square Garden was the center of the college basketball universe then, hosting frequent doubleheaders, the NIT and seven of the first 12 NCAA tournaments. The city's schools also prospered, often with dominant African-Americans, the first of whom was LIU's Dolly King. He once played a collegiate football game in the afternoon (he caught a touchdown pass) and a basketball game at the Garden that evening, both under legendary coach Clair Bee.

World War II had less effect on college basketball than on other sports—many centers and forwards were too big to draft—and so it was that a bespectacled giant named George Mikan materialized at DePaul in Chicago to dominate the mid-decade. As the '50s crept near, British astronomer Fred Hoyle coined the term "Big Bang," and college basketball was about to feel a seismic jolt itself. —J.M.

> All-Decade Teams

FIRST TEAM

Ralph Beard
G - KENTUCKY

Andy Phillip
G - ILLINOIS

Ed Macauley
F - SAINT LOUIS

Bob Kurland
F - OKLAHOMA A&M

George Mikan
C - DEPAUL

SECOND TEAM

Bob Cousy
G - HOLY CROSS

Stan Modzelewski
G - RHODE ISLAND

Leo Klier
F - NOTRE DAME

Paul Arizin
F - VILLANOVA

Alex Groza
C - KENTUCKY

Oregon's Bob Anet (20) receives the '39 championship trophy.

	NATIONAL CHAMPION	COACH	SCORING LEADER	POINTS PER GAME
'39*	**OREGON**	Howard Hobson	**CHESTER JAWORSKI,** Rhode Island	22.6
'40	**INDIANA**	Branch McCracken	**STAN MODZELEWSKI,** Rhode Island	23.1
'41	**WISCONSIN**	Harold (Bud) Foster	**STAN MODZELEWSKI,** Rhode Island	18.5
'42	**STANFORD**	Everett Dean	**STAN MODZELEWSKI,** Rhode Island	21.4
'43	**WYOMING**	Everett Shelton	**GEORGE SENESKY,** St. Joseph's	23.4
'44	**UTAH**	Vadal Peterson	**ERNIE CALVERLEY,** Rhode Island	26.7
'45	**OKLAHOMA STATE**	Henry Iba	**GEORGE MIKAN,** DePaul	23.3
'46	**OKLAHOMA STATE**	Henry Iba	**GEORGE MIKAN,** DePaul	23.1
'47	**HOLY CROSS**	Alvin (Doggie) Julian	**JIM LACY,** Loyola (Md.)	20.8
'48	**KENTUCKY**	Adolph Rupp	**MURRAY WIER,** Iowa	21.0
'49	**KENTUCKY**	Adolph Rupp	**TONY LAVELLI,** Yale	22.4

*DENOTES YEAR IN WHICH SEASON ENDED

>> WISH YOU WERE THERE

Yale 32, Penn 10

MARCH 20, 1897 • YALE GYMNASIUM, NEW HAVEN, CONN.
The Elis and Quakers meet in what is considered by most historians to be the first intercollegiate game played with five players a side. It is also thought to be the first time a fee is charged to attend a basketball game, as 800 fans pay 35 cents each for a ticket.

Temple 60, Colorado 36

MARCH 16, 1938 • MADISON SQUARE GARDEN Looking to crown a true college basketball champion, the New York Metropolitan Basketball Writers Association invites six teams to participate in the first National Invitation Tournament. Owls MVP Don Shields scores 16 points in the title-game rout of the Buffaloes, whose second-leading scorer, with 10 points, is future Supreme Court Justice Byron (Whizzer) White.

Wyoming 52, St. John's 47 (OT)

APRIL 1, 1943 • MADISON SQUARE GARDEN To raise money for the wartime Red Cross, a game is arranged between the winner of the NCAA tournament, Wyoming, and NIT winner St. John's. Making his final appearance before starting a two-year stint in the Marines, Ken Sailors of Wyoming, the player often credited as being the

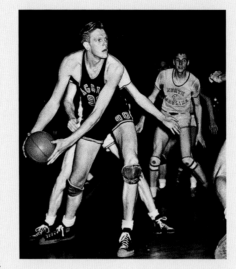

creator of the jump shot, goes coast-to-coast for the game-winner at the buzzer—only to have it disallowed. The refs rule that St. John's had called time after making the game-tying basket with :05 left, capping a furious comeback from eight points down in the final two minutes. The Cowboys prevail in OT, though, to stake their claim as undisputed champs.

< Okla. A&M 43, North Carolina 40

MARCH 26, 1946 • MADISON SQUARE GARDEN
Bob Kurland *(with ball)*, the 7-foot star for coach Hank Iba's Aggies, puts on a show in his final collegiate game, scoring 23 points to lead A&M to the first repeat as NCAA tournament champions. The first dominant big man in tournament history, Kurland scores 72 of the Aggies' 139 total points in the NCAAs.

Oklahoma 55, Texas 54

MARCH 22, 1947 • MUNICIPAL AUDITORIUM, KANSAS CITY, MO. Ken Pryor, who had missed the previous two seasons while in the Navy, takes his only shot of the 1947 NCAA tournament, with seven seconds left in the semifinal, and it is huge. He banks in a two-handed set shot to send Oklahoma to the title game against Holy Cross.

GAME CHANGER

NAT HOLMAN
THE GIVE AND GO

Coach of CCNY for 37 seasons before his retirement in 1960, Holman built this ingeniously simple attack with snappy passes and strong screens. The point guard (1, left) delivers the ball to a forward (3), then cuts hard to the goal for a return pass (middle). Meanwhile, the shooting guard (2), having curled around picks on the baseline (middle), is also ready to receive a pass (right). If the defender on the forward (3, right) sloughs off him, the forward will have an open shot.

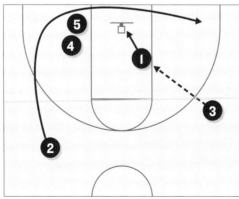
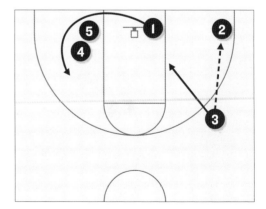

PASS ---------->   CUT ————>   1: PG 2: SG 3: SF 4: PF 5: C

>> TIME CAPSULE

THE MAN The nation's top scorer in 1935–36 and '36–37, Stanford's Hank Luisetti was the first player to regularly leave his feet while shooting, using his patented running one-handed shot. The 6' 2" forward's slashing style led to never-before-seen scoring totals, highlighted by a 50-point game—the first of its kind—in a 92–27 win over Duquesne in 1938.

THE WOMAN The sister of art historian Bernard Berenson (and great-great aunt of actress Marisa) seems an unlikely figure to be considered the mother of women's college basketball, but Senda Berenson earned that distinction by introducing the women's game at Smith College in 1893 and writing the rule book that grew the game on the distaff side.

THE CINDERELLA The 1944 Utah team may be the unlikeliest NCAA champion ever. The Utes weren't in the original tournament field; they went to the NIT instead and lost there. But a terrible car accident forced Arkansas to withdraw from the NCAAs and Utah took the Hogs' place and won the whole thing. They then beat the NIT champs, St. John's, in a special Red Cross benefit game at Madison Square Garden.

The look of cheerleading at N.C. State in 1946.

THE STREAK With eight Eastern Collegiate League titles and two trips to the Final Four before 1946, Dartmouth was an early power in the ranks of college hoops. But the Big Green didn't win a single game from March 6, 1917 until Jan. 10, 1920, a stretch that reached 34 straight defeats. Dartmouth's 26 losses in 1917–18 would stand as an NCAA record for most defeats in a single winless season until Prairie View A&M put up a 0–28 mark in 1991–92.

BASKETBALL BABYLON
THE FIX WAS IN

Riding a 22-game winning streak into the opening game of the 1949 NIT, top-ranked and heavily favored Kentucky inexplicably fell to Loyola of Chicago 67–56. An investigation later discovered that this was one of 86 games in 33 cities influenced by gamblers between 1947 and '50. In the aftermath Kentucky would be banned from play for the '52–53 season, and Wildcats star center Alex Groza (*middle*), guard Ralph Beard (*to Groza's right*) and guard Dale Barnstable, all then in the NBA, would be indicted for point shaving. They would each admit to accepting $500 in bribes and receive suspended sentences but were banned from the NBA for life.

> BY THE NUMBERS

148 Points scored in 12 league games by UCLA's Jackie Robinson in 1940 to lead the Pacific Coast Conference. Seven years later he would break baseball's color barrier with the Dodgers.

2 Total number of weeks spent at No. 1 in the 1949 AP poll by Saint Louis. The Billikens earned the No. 1 spot in the very first poll, released on Jan. 18, held it one more week, and have yet to return to No. 1 again.

31 Age at which Branch McCracken coached Indiana to a national championship in 1940. It is still an NCAA record.

14 Minutes played by DePaul's 6' 9" center George Mikan against Oklahoma A&M's 7-foot Bob Kurland in the much anticipated 1945 Red Cross Benefit Game. Mikan fouled out with nine points, to Kurland's 14, as the Aggies won easily, 52–44.

2 Games, Fordham vs. Pittsburgh and NYU vs. Georgetown, shown in the first TV broadcast of college basketball, on Feb. 28, 1940.

2002 | PHILLY'S PALESTRA rocked to the thumping baseline play of Penn's Andrew Toole (20) and Yale's Alex Gamboa (20) in a battle for Ivy laurels. | *Photograph by* MANNY MILLAN

1974 | BILL WALTON, a three-time player of the year at UCLA, had his game face on as he crashed the boards against crosstown rival USC. | *Photograph by* LONG PHOTOGRAPHY

1974 | DAVID THOMPSON defied gravity and the efforts of two helpless Maryland defenders as he led N.C. State to an ACC tournament title. | *Photograph by* JOHN D. HANLON

A FULL FLOWERING IN THE GARDEN

BY ROY TERRELL

College basketball on TV is a relatively recent development. Even a star like Bill Russell, who'd won a national championship as a junior, was a mystery to East Coast fans—till he came to New York as a senior and showed what he could do. —from SI, JANUARY 9, 1956

FROM THE MOMENT, AS AN ALMOST unknown junior, that Bill Russell began to lead San Francisco into national prominence last season, people have been writing and talking about this amazing string bean and his phenomenal feats. From the West Coast the word filtered across the mountains last year that here was a basketball "find," one of the real giants of the game; by March, when the Dons beat Tom Gola and La Salle in Kansas City for the NCAA championship, Bill Russell was accepted nearly everywhere as the best player in the nation.

There remained, however, a hard core of nonbelievers; or, if not nonbelievers, at least a group willing to be convinced but determined to first see with their own eyes before passing judgment for themselves: the aficionados of Madison Square Garden who, through the years, have watched men like Luisetti and Mikan and Cousy and Macauley and Gola perform their magic and are seldom convinced by mere words alone. So last week, as coach Phil Woolpert of San Francisco brought the nation's No. 1 team—and No. 1 player—into New York for the annual Holiday Festival Tournament, the crowds packed the big sports arena from the sidelines to the ceiling to see for themselves.

At first they greeted Russell with a stubborn silence. Then, when he failed to shoot like a Carl Braun or dribble like a Bob Cousy or feed like a Dick McGuire, their silence changed to hoots and jeers for this big shuffling man who was so evidently not a complete basketball player. On offense he ambled lazily to a spot near the free throw lane, almost reluctantly took passes from his teammates and quickly shoveled the ball to someone else. And finally, when his defender strayed away to ponder from a distance the incongruity of this All-America who wouldn't shoot, Russell did begin to shoot from a distance of a dozen feet—and missed badly, not once, not twice, but three straight times, easy little shots that any good basketball player could sink. What then, asked the crowd, can he do?

Russell showed them. As the tournament progressed, the looks of doubt and derision changed into looks of incredulity and awe. For the things which Russell can do he does superlatively well, perhaps better than anyone has ever done them before.

Physically he is 6' 10", has such amazing spring that he high jumps over 6' 7" and has the speed to cover a court like a late-evening shadow. His arms are tremendously long, even for a man of such height, and he has the reactions of a featherweight fighter—quickness and timing—and great competitive spirit beneath an almost phlegmatic exterior.

What the Garden crowds saw was a player who could drop off his man on one side of the court, take two immense strides and block a shot by an opposing forward flashing in unguarded from the opposite side of the court. They saw a player who could come down with 62 rebounds against magnificent athletes like 6' 7" Tom Heinsohn of Holy Cross and 6' 5" Willie Naulls of UCLA. A player who went up, time and again, to pluck a wild shot by a teammate from the backboard and cram it down through the basket. A player who (although he couldn't hit from outside) was deadly on soft little hook shots right under the basket; who batted so many seemingly sure shots away from the basket it was discouraging (and psychologically unnerving) to anyone with a goal-shooting gleam in his eye.

Without Russell, San Francisco's 33-game victory streak would never have survived the first round of the Garden tournament. The Dons trailed La Salle until the big fellow began to wage a one-man war under the basket, finally emerging with 22 rebounds, 26 points and a fistful of blocked shots. San Francisco won 79–62. Against Holy Cross in the semis Russell outplayed Heinsohn in one of the stirring man-to-man duels of Garden basketball history. In the opener against Syracuse, Heinsohn had scored 36 points; Russell stopped him with 12, scored 24 himself, had 22 rebounds and batted away half a dozen shots. San Francisco won 67–51.

In the finals, K. C. Jones and the rest of the San Francisco lineup ran rings around UCLA, outshot the Bruins, outrebounded them, and won 70–53. Russell, under no pressure to come through with another big performance, took things easy. Even so he seized 18 rebounds, scored 17 points and earned an overwhelming vote as the tournament's outstanding player....

RUSSELL HAD an awkward-looking shot, but he was a terror under the basket at both ends of the court.

1969 | LEW ALCINDOR was literally head and shoulders above his classmates at graduation, and figuratively so among his peers on the court. | *Photograph by* CURT GUNTHER

1985 | MUGGSY BOGUES might have been just 5′ 3″, but he ruled the court at Wake Forest, averaging 13.1 points and 8.9 assists his final two seasons. | *Photograph by* SUSAN WEINIK

2008 | CARDINAL VIRTUES were apparent in a Stanford victory as Robin Lopez (42) and his twin brother, Brook, each put a body on an Oregon rebounder. | *Photograph by* DAVID GONZALES

AN UNRIVALED RIVALRY

BY ALEXANDER WOLFF

The campuses are only eight miles apart but an endless enmity separates Duke and North Carolina, two schools that have title dreams nearly every year but want nothing more than to beat each other.   —from SI, MARCH 6, 1995

ART HEYMAN WAS AN innocent when he left Long Island for the Triangle of North Carolina 35 years ago. A saint, no—Heyman played basketball and lived life with a hard-to-the-hole swagger—but a naïf just the same. Duke? North Carolina? Heyman could barely tell a Tar Devil from a Blue Heel when he arrived at Raleigh-Durham Airport to play ball for. . . .

Well, he was going to play for North Carolina. He had even signed a grant-in-aid to attend Chapel Hill. But that was before his campus visit, during which his stepfather said something about Tar Heels coach Frank McGuire running "a factory," and McGuire took offense, and Heyman had to keep the two men from throwing punches at each other.

So Heyman wound up going to Duke, where Vic Bubas had just taken over as coach. "My friends from New York, Larry Brown and Doug Moe, they were at Carolina," Heyman says today. "If Duke hadn't been there to pick me up at the airport, I would have just gone down the road and started school there."

He soon learned that there is no such thing as "just going down" Tobacco Road. In a freshman game against Carolina, Moe, Heyman's supposed friend, spat at him. The next season, with Heyman now playing on the Blue Devils varsity, Brown, who would have been his roommate in Chapel Hill, engaged him in fisticuffs, which escalated into a brawl that required 10 cops to restore peace. A Durham lawyer with ties to the Tar Heels would swear out an assault warrant against Heyman over an altercation with a North Carolina male cheerleader during the brawl. And Heyman believes private detectives hired by Tar Heels partisans tailed him for the rest of his career, which may explain why as a senior he was arrested at a Myrtle Beach, S.C., motel—where he and a lady friend had checked in as Mr. and Mrs. Oscar Robertson—and charged with transporting a woman across state lines for immoral purposes.

By the time he was named national Player of the Year in 1963, Heyman had been vilified, castigated and pilloried, all in the name of shades of blue. To be sure, there had been earlier flare-ups in this neighborhood feud; when the Blue Devils beat up on McGuire's first teams, in the early 1950s, Duke students mocked the Tar Heel coach by slicking back their hair and donning silly ties. The rivalry would stagnate somewhat during the early 1980s, when the Tar Heels' dominance helped them build what's currently a 115–78 overall lead in the series. But the feud heated up again with the Blue Devils' resurgence later in the decade, and today nothing quite compares to what happens when Duke tips off against North Carolina.

Between them the two schools have won four NCAA titles in 13 years and three of the last four. They account for six of the 20 spots in the last five Final Fours. In the trigonometry of the Triangle that encompasses Chapel Hill, Durham and Raleigh (home of N.C. State), Duke and Carolina are straight lines forming a right angle; you won't find their players on public assistance 10 years out or the schools' names in the police blotter of *The NCAA News*. Like Gore Vidal and Norman Mailer, the two teams can cut each other up in public and then retreat to their adjacent villas and their snifters of brandy, content that they're the very best at what they do.

Last season they met when ranked one-two in the AP poll, and there ensued an appropriately terrific game won by No. 2 North Carolina 89–78. But on Feb. 2 of this season, with the Blue Devils an uncharacteristic 0–7 in the ACC and their coach, Mike Krzyzewski, out for the year with a bad back, and the second-ranked Tar Heels heavily favored, they played an even better game: a 102–100 double-overtime epic of which the winning coach, Carolina's Dean Smith, who has seen a lot, said, "I've never seen anything like it."

That night, a Duke assistant coach says, he witnessed three of the best plays he has ever seen college players make: 6' 6" Tar Heel Jerry Stackhouse's in-transition flight past one Duke big man, Cherokee Parks, and over another, Erik Meek, to the far side of the rim for a reverse jam; a tap dunk in traffic by North Carolina's 6' 10" Rasheed Wallace; and Parks's block of a dunk attempt by Stackhouse in the final minute of regulation. All three plays were incidental to the evening's greater drama, which actually made ESPN2 color commentator Dick Vitale's hyperventilations seem . . . *considered.* Animated by excellence, informed by tradition and stoked by proximity, Duke versus North Carolina stands as the one rivalry all other rivalries secretly wish to be. . . .

VIRTUALLY ALL Duke–North Carolina games are as hotly contested as this 1995 play in which Wallace (center) posterized a trio of Blue Devil defenders.

2002 | A TRANSITIONAL moment occurred as UConn's Taliek Brown (12) grabbed a loose ball and readied the Husky break against Arizona. | *Photograph by* ROBERT BECK

1961 | AS A buttoned-up, buckled-in Buckeye, Jerry Lucas averaged 24.3 points and 17.2 boards for three seasons, leading Ohio State to three Final Fours and a title. | *Photograph by* NEIL LEIFER

2011 | ORANGE BLOSSOMS every time Syracuse takes the floor at the Carrier Dome, where a season-high, up-in-arms crowd of 33,736 greeted Villanova. | *Photograph by* FRED VUICH

THE TWO FACES OF THE RUBBER MAN

BY JOE JARES

John Wooden became known as perhaps the greatest coach of all time, but that shouldn't obscure his legacy as one of the college game's first star players. —*from* SI, JANUARY 6, 1969

H E HAD A WAY OF TAKING off near the foul line and sailing up to the basket "as smooth and pretty as a bird." Or he would drive in for a layup with such determination that his momentum would carry him into the fifth row of the school band at the end of the court. He bounced off the floor so often that people called him the India Rubber Man.

That was John Wooden 35 or 40 years ago. Today he is known mainly as the coach at UCLA—the lucky man who won the Lew Alcindor recruiting sweepstakes and thus practically sewed up three straight NCAA championships for the Bruins. And that in a way is a shame. So obscured is he by the telephone-pole shadow cast by his center that only the few fanatics who keep the *Encyclopedia of Basketball* out on their coffee tables seem to know there is a niche—maybe even a whole room—reserved for John Wooden in the sport's Hall of Fame.

Wooden was an outstanding professional player for six years. Before that he was a consensus All-America guard at Purdue for three straight seasons. And before that he starred on one of the finest high school teams ever to play in Indiana. As a coach he has had only one losing season, his first. His UCLA teams won two national titles before Alcindor, and they are likely to win some more after he leaves.

Away from games, the former India Rubber Man is a soft-spoken gentleman with a trace of homespun Hoosier in his voice, a human *Poor Richard's Almanack* who has inspirational sayings filed in a loose-leaf notebook, taped to his pencil box, framed on his walls, tucked away in his wallet. Somewhere between "Be true to yourself" and "It's the little things that count," a visitor begins to think it is all just a giant put-on. Nobody could be that square. But Wooden is real all right, sitting there in his office overlooking UCLA's new basketball palace, Pauley Pavilion.

When Wooden gets off a small joke or receives a compliment, he does not flash a white-neon smile, he ducks his head and grins sheepishly. It is easy to imagine him as a deacon of his church or a kindly grandfather, both of which he is. Not so easy to imagine, but real nevertheless, is the intensely competitive John Wooden of the Bruins bench whose angry, sometimes scathing comments can melt a referee's whistle in mid-tweet.

"I've seen him so mad that I've been afraid he'd pop that big blood vessel in his forehead," says a Pacific Coast official, "but I've never heard him curse."

John Robert Wooden grew up on a farm eight miles from Martinsville, Ind. His father, Joshua, who never had much money or good fortune, was a pretty good pitcher and built a diamond among the wheat, corn and alfalfa. To this day baseball, not basketball, is Wooden's favorite sport. But there also was a hoop nailed up in the hayloft, and he and his older brother, Maurice, played there with any kind of ball they could find.

John attended the four-room Centerton grade school, where he was the star athlete. Centerton's principal, Earl Warriner, was one of the important influences on his life. Once, when John was being recalcitrant, Warriner, who also coached basketball, allowed his high scorer to sit out an entire losing game. "After it was over," said Wooden, "he put an arm on my shoulder and said 'Johnny, we could have won with you in there, but winning just isn't that important.'"

Wooden's dad lost the farm because of some bad investments and the Woodens moved into Martinsville in 1924, at about the same time the red brick high school gym was built on South Main Street. The population of the town was 5,200 and the gym held, as noted at the time in *Ripley's Believe It or Not*, 5,520. John Bob soon made the transition from hayseed to sharp dude, Central Indiana version. Hanging around with his buddies at Wick's Candy Kitchen, he wore his letterman's sweater and a green hat Maurice had brought home from Franklin College. He usually had a toothpick in his mouth.

John Bob always worked hard—digging sewers one summer—and he was a good student, but, as longtime friend Floyd Burns remembered, "He always had time for basketball, baseball and Nellie Riley." Nell played the trumpet in the school band and John, as a sophomore in 1926, got in the habit of winking at her before each game. He's still doing it more than 40 years later. . . .

BEFORE HE began practicing his wizardry in Westwood, Wooden was the game's first-ever three-time consensus All-America, at Purdue from 1929 to '32.

2001 | THE BOILERMAKERS' Katie Douglas got a shot (but no beer) from Final Four Cinderella Southwest Missouri State in Purdue's semifinal win. | *Photograph by* AL TIELEMANS

2009 | A SHOW of hands illustrated the physical play as UConn's Jeff Adrien (4) tussled with Missouri's J.T. Tiller in the West Regional final. | *Photograph by* JOHN W. MCDONOUGH

1979 | MAGIC JOHNSON was all smiles when he got together with Larry Bird before their championship-game showdown in
Salt Lake City, and he had the last laugh when the fiercely contested final was over. | *Photographs by* JEROME MCLENDON *(above) and* JAMES DRAKE

EYES OF THE STORM

BY GARY SMITH

With 1,071 career wins, 18 Final Four appearances and eight national titles, Pat Summitt has proven herself to be the greatest women's coach of all time; the way she's done it shows she's also a force of nature. —from SI, MARCH 2, 1998

HERE COMES THIS LADY INTO your life. You don't know that she has been up all night peeing, racked with pain in her lower back. You don't know how many people told her she was nuts to get on an airplane and fly to your hometown at a time like this. You don't know that an hour ago, when her water broke, she was crouched in an eight-seat King Air blotting her legs with paper towels. Hell, you're 16. You don't know that she's spitting Nature in the eye and kicking Time in the teeth.

She's sitting on your sofa as you come through the door on a September day in 1990, and she grins and grinds her teeth against the contractions. Michelle Marciniak takes a seat and looks around her living room. She's a senior at Allentown (Pa.) Central Catholic High, an hour north of Philadelphia, a guard who in six months will become the Naismith and Gatorade player of the year. Her mom, Betsy, and her older brother, Steve, are wearing the same nervous, crooked little smile. Pat's bouncing from the sofa to the bathroom to the telephone and back. Her assistant coach, Mickie DeMoss, is whipping through Tennessee's recruiting scrapbook as if she were sitting on a mound of fire ants: Here's the arena, here's the library, here's the '89 national championship—O.K., Michelle, any questions?

Suddenly Nature mounts a furious comeback, Time starts kicking Pat in the teeth. "Mickie," she blurts, "we have to go. Now." Suddenly they're babbling to the teenage girl that Pat's baby is coming, and Steve and Michelle are racing to his car to lead the Tennessee coaches to—to the hospital, right?—heck no, to the airport, because Patricia Head Summitt is going to have this baby when and where she wants it. They screech to a halt near the airport's private hangars. "I'll call you!" Pat shouts to Michelle. She strides into the King Air, and off she roars into the sky.

Let's dash right past the next three years; let's bully Time, the way Pat does. Let's fly by the day Pat throws her point guard out of practice in her junior year, past the day when Michelle finally crumbles and sobs in front of everyone. Let's jump clean over the last day of that same junior year, when Michelle comes within a whisker of her dream but loses in the NCAA title game to Connecticut—still unsure of herself in critical moments, no longer the All-America guard nor even the all-conference one.

It's February 1996. Time's not ticking now for Pat and Michelle. It's hammering. Pat has won national titles in '87, '89 and '91, but four years have elapsed since her last one, and she needs her team leader, Michelle, as much as Michelle needs her.

Michelle's desperate. It's her last shot at the title, her last shot to regain the kind of national acclaim that vanished for her after high school. But how can she? The 17–3 Lady Vols look nothing like a title team—and guess whose fault that is?

Now Pat's team has gotten skunked a fourth time, by Mississippi, and Michelle has gone 0 for 7 from the field and fouled out. The bus is crawling toward the airport as Pat rises and takes a seat next to Michelle and tells her that unless something drastic happens, she doesn't think the Lady Vols can win a title with Michelle as their point guard. Pat has already brought Michelle to tears twice that day, at halftime and just after the game, and . . . here it . . . here it comes . . . the third wave of sobs.

Michelle doesn't sleep that night. She's terrified. The girl with the brightest flame is dead inside. She cannot. Take this. Anymore.

At 6:45 a.m. she calls Pat's home. Only fear and despair could make her speak to Pat Summitt this way: "You don't think we can win it all with me playing like I am," she says, "but I . . . I don't think we can win it all with you coaching like you are. You've got to back off me."

Maybe it's because Pat has won so many championships that she can be more flexible now. Maybe Pat has no real choice this late in the season. She and Michelle speak for a while, and then there's silence. Well? "Doesn't mean I won't criticize you anymore, do you understand?" Pat says. "But I'll try it."

With that, everything changes. "As if we were two people in a room with boxing gloves," Michelle will say later, "who finally both come out with our hands up." Pat gives Michelle more rope. Michelle quits trying to tie a triple knot when a single will do just fine. Tennessee reels off 15 straight wins, beating UConn in OT in the NCAA semifinals behind Michelle's 21 points and then blowing out Georgia to win the crown.

Pat gets the first hug and kiss from her father that she can remember. Michelle is chosen the Final Four MVP. Her flying leap into Pat's arms nearly knocks Pat off her feet. . . .

THE FAMOUS Summitt stare is what Tennessee players face after a careless pass or an unthinking shot, and it has helped bring eight NCAA titles to Knoxville.

2003 | A TEXAS-OKLAHOMA game can be just as physical on the court as on the gridiron, as the Sooners' Jabahri Brown learned when he tried to go to the rack. | *Photograph by* JOHN BIEVER

1995 | RAY ALLEN grew up as an Air Force brat and, coincidentally or not, developed into one of the game's greatest long-range shooters at UConn. | *Photograph by* JEFFREY LOWE

1983 | MICHAEL JORDAN (top, right) and Sam Perkins clowned around off the court, but they were all business on it, winning an NCAA title in '82. | *Photograph by* LANE STEWART

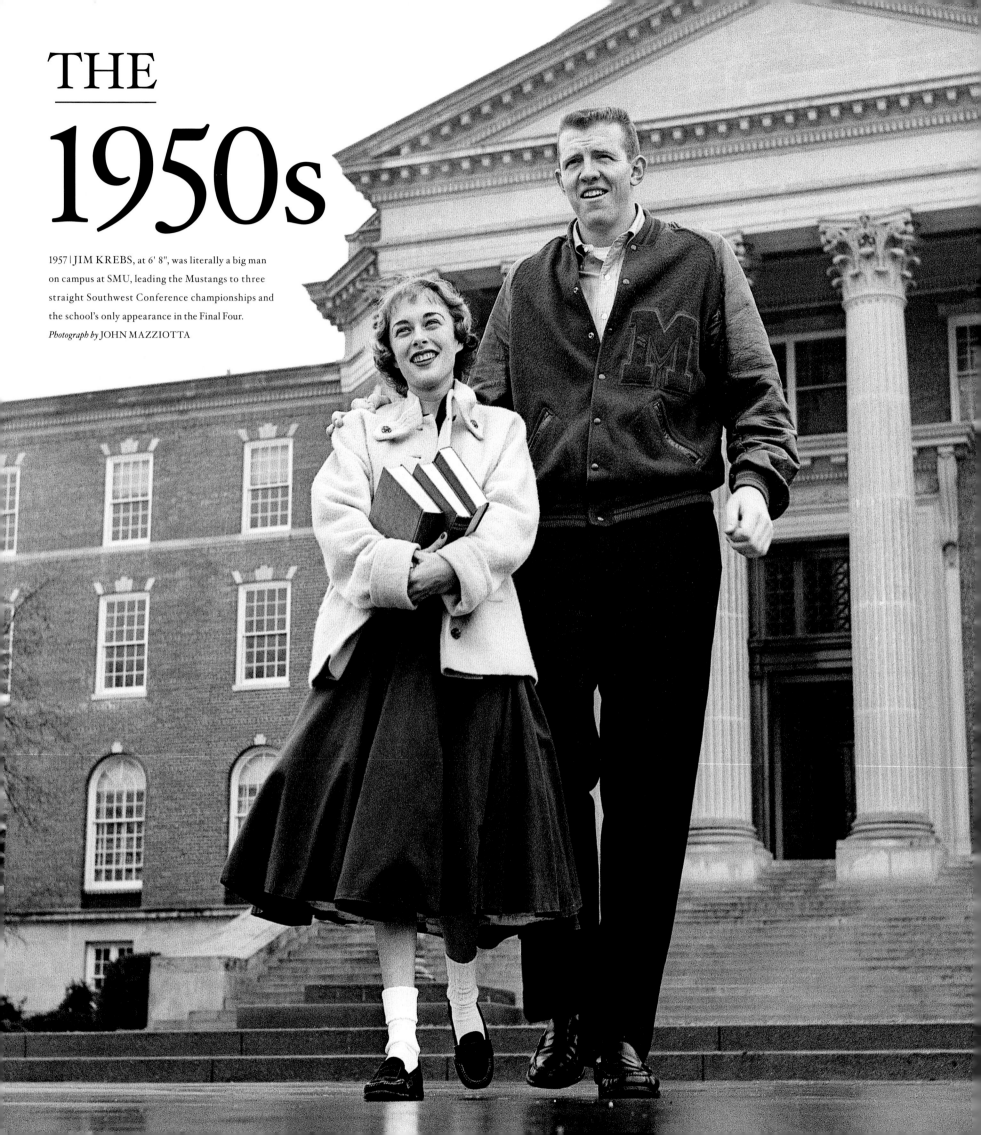

THE
1950s

1957 | JIM KREBS, at 6' 8", was literally a big man on campus at SMU, leading the Mustangs to three straight Southwest Conference championships and the school's only appearance in the Final Four.
Photograph by JOHN MAZZIOTTA

>> BIRTH AND REBIRTH

NOT LONG AFTER TENNESSEE DEMOCRAT Estes Kefauver convened the first Congressional hearings on organized crime in 1950, the sound of his gavel reverberated throughout college hoops. By the winter of 1951, New York district attorney Frank Hogan had arrested 32 players from seven colleges who had conspired to fix games, including three Wildcats from Kentucky, whose coach, the crusty Adolph Rupp, had observed that "[Gamblers] couldn't touch my boys with a 10-foot pole."

But as the decade wore on, people began to forgive the game and its transgressors, probably because they were distracted by so many other things. The unclothed women in a new magazine called *Playboy*. The real-life birth of Desi Arnaz Jr., which was written into the plotline of *I Love Lucy*. Joe DiMaggio's doomed marriage to Marilyn Monroe. And, of course, Elvis's pelvis, carried live by Ed Sullivan. There were tears when Buddy Holly, Richie Valens and the Big Bopper went down in an Iowa cornfield in 1959, but the music didn't really die—that same year Miles Davis released *Kind of Blue*, and a songwriter named Berry Gordy Jr. started a label called Motown.

So by the time that Cincinnati's Oscar Robertson and West Virginia's Jerry West came along at the tail end of the decade, America had begun to look a lot like the country it is today, with McDonald's and Holiday Inns beginning to dot the horizon, a magic place called Disneyland to visit, and Alaska and Hawaii giving us an even 50 states.   —J.M.

Desi and Lucy welcomed Desi Jr. in '53.

> All-Decade Teams

FIRST TEAM

Jerry West
G - WEST VIRGINIA

Oscar Robertson
G - CINCINNATI

Elgin Baylor
F - SEATTLE

Tom Gola
F - LaSALLE

Bill Russell
C - SAN FRANCISCO

SECOND TEAM

Guy Rodgers
G - TEMPLE

Sihugo Green
G - DUQUESNE

Bob Boozer
F - KANSAS STATE

Bailey Howell
F - MISSISSIPPI STATE

Wilt Chamberlain
C - KANSAS

NATIONAL CHAMPION

		COACH
'50*	CCNY	Nat Holman
'51	KENTUCKY	Adolph Rupp
'52	KANSAS	Phog Allen
'53	INDIANA	Branch McCracken
'54	LaSALLE	Ken Loeffler
'55	SAN FRANCISCO	Phil Woolpert
'56	SAN FRANCISCO	Phil Woolpert
'57	NORTH CAROLINA	Frank McGuire
'58	KENTUCKY	Adolph Rupp
'59	CALIFORNIA	Pete Newell

LEADING SCORER

	POINTS PER GAME
PAUL ARIZIN, Villanova	25.3
BILL MLKVY, Temple	29.2
CLYDE LOVELLETTE, Kansas	28.6
FRANK SELVY, Furman	29.5
FRANK SELVY, Furman	41.7
DARRELL FLOYD, Furman	35.9
DARRELL FLOYD, Furman	33.8
GRADY WALLACE, South Carolina	31.2
OSCAR ROBERTSON, Cincinnati	35.1
OSCAR ROBERTSON, Cincinnati	32.6

LEADING REBOUNDER

	REBOUNDS PER GAME
ERNIE BECK, Penn	20.6
BILL HANNON, Army	20.9
ED CONLIN, Fordham	23.5
ART QUIMBY, Connecticut	22.6
CHARLIE SLACK, Marshall	25.6
JOE HOLUP, George Washington	256**
ELGIN BAYLOR, Seattle	235**
ALEX (BOO) ELLIS, Niagara	262**
LEROY WRIGHT, Pacific	238**

*DENOTES YEAR IN WHICH SEASON ENDED **LEADER DETERMINED BY PERCENTAGE OF BOTH TEAMS' REBOUNDS

>> WISH YOU WERE THERE

Duke 74, Tulane 72

DECEMBER 30, 1950 • REYNOLDS COLISEUM, RALEIGH
Trailing by as many as 32 points in the first half and by 56–27 at halftime, Duke completes the largest single-game turnaround in college basketball history as future major league baseball star Dick Groat scores 25 of his game-high 32 points in the second half. Tulane doesn't score a single point in the game's final eight minutes.

San Francisco 57, Oregon State 56

MARCH 12, 1955 • GILL COLISEUM, CORVALLIS, ORE.
Bill Russell's Dons are in control of the West Regional final with an eight-point lead and a minute to go when 7' 3" Swede Halbrook scores five quick points in a 7–1 Beaver run. A free throw after a technical on the Dons' K.C. Jones makes it a one-point game, but a wide-open potential game-winning try from the corner by sharpshooter Ron Robins rims out.

North Carolina 74, Michigan State 70 (3OT)

MARCH 22, 1957 • MUNICIPAL AUDITORIUM, KANSAS CITY, MO. The Spartans' Jack Quiggle hits a 50-foot prayer at the end of regulation but the refs rule that time had expired. At the end of the first OT,

State's Johnny Green misses the front end of a one-and-one to ice the game, and Pete Brennan hits a 20-footer at the horn to launch a second OT. The Heels' Lennie Rosenbluth puts the game away in the third OT with two steals and two baskets.

North Carolina 54, Kansas 53 (3OT)

MARCH 23, 1957 • MUNICIPAL AUDITORIUM, KANSAS CITY, MO.
Fresh off that three-overtime thriller less than 24 hours earlier, the undefeated Tar Heels go another three OTs to beat Wilt Chamberlain and Kansas as Tar Heels center Joe Quigg hits the deciding free throws with six seconds left.

<California 71, West Virginia 70

MARCH 21, 1959 • FREEDOM HALL, LOUISVILLE
Junior center Darrall Imhoff, who came to Cal as a walk-on and became an All-America under coach Pete Newell, scores the deciding points in a thrilling title game when he tips in his own missed hook shot with 17 seconds to go. The upset win over the Mountaineers comes despite the heroics of two-time All-America Jerry West *(above)*, who is named Most Outstanding Player after scoring a record-tying 160 points in the five-game tournament.

GAME CHANGER
ADOLPH RUPP
THE SINGLE-PIVOT POST

In choreographing his Kentucky Wildcats' attack, the Baron of the Bluegrass reached back to an offensive set devised by the barnstorming Original Celtics in which a team's movement revolves around its big man (5), who posts up on the low block and receives the ball on a pass *(left)*. His teammates then cut around him and set screens *(middle)*. The pivotman can pitch to an open man *(right)* or put up a shot himself.

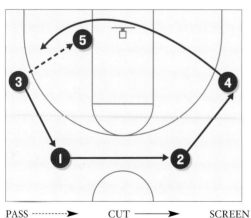

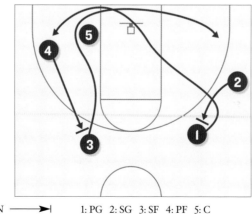

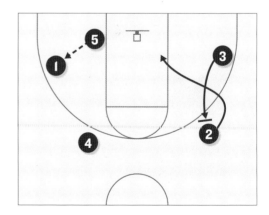

PASS ---------->   CUT ——→   SCREEN ——→| 1: PG   2: SG   3: SF   4: PF   5: C

>> TIME CAPSULE

THE MAN Probably no player in college history rose from greater obscurity to such heights as Bill Russell. Playing for the University of San Francisco—the only school to offer him a scholarship—the 6' 9" center became the first of only five Division I players to average 20 points and 20 rebounds (20.7 points, 20.3 boards) over an entire career, leading the Dons to back-to-back national championships in 1955 and '56.

THE WOMAN A great shooter, passer and dribbler, 6' 1" Nera White was years ahead of her time. She played for the Nashville Business College AAU team because the George Peabody College for Teachers in Nashville (now part of Vanderbilt), had no team, and in 1957–58 she led the U.S. to a title in the World Championships in Brazil and was named MVP of the tournament. She was inducted in the Basketball Hall of Fame in 1992.

THE STREAK The women of Wayland Baptist College also played on the AAU circuit, and after losing the 1953 AAU title game, the Flying Queens—their nickname because benefactor Claude Hutcherson would pilot them to out-of-town games via airplane— didn't lose again until the semis of the 1958 tournament, a stretch in which they won 131 games and four national titles.

THE CINDERELLA Coach Nat Holman's '49–50 CCNY team had one of the greatest March runs ever. The Beavers beat defending NIT champ San Francisco, defending NCAA champ Kentucky, sixth-ranked Duquesne and top-ranked Bradley to win the NIT. Then in the NCAAs, CCNY defeated second-ranked Ohio State, fifth-ranked N.C. State and Bradley again to become the only team ever to win both the NCAA and the NIT in the same season.

The '50s look at Cal: saddle shoes and pleats.

BASKETBALL BABYLON
A BLIGHT OF BETTORS

If there was any thought that busting the point-shaving ring of the late '40s had cleaned up the game for good, Jack Molinas (middle) put an end to that notion. The 6' 6" former Columbia standout masterminded an even more widespread and damaging scheme, lining up players from 27 schools to manipulate the results of at least 43 games between 1957 and '61. Foremost among the players whose careers were damaged by their association with Molinas was Connie Hawkins, who lost his scholarship at Iowa before ever playing a varsity game there, despite even Molinas's insistence that Hawkins never shaved points.

> BY THE NUMBERS

116 | Points scored by Clarence (Bevo) Francis of Division II Rio Grande against Ashland College, a two-year school, on Jan. 9, 1953. A year later the 6' 9" Francis would score 113 against Hillsdale to set the record between four-year schools.

100 | Points scored by Furman's Frank Selvy against Newberry on Feb. 13, 1954, the last two on a 40-footer with time expiring. It's the only time a Division I player has reached triple digits.

1 | NCAA scoring leaders who have also won an NCAA title the same year. Kansas's Clyde Lovellette did it in 1951–52.

500 | Approximate enrollment at Lebanon Valley College, which beat Fordham in the 1953 NCAAs. It is the smallest school ever to advance to the Sweet 16.

51 | Rebounds grabbed by William & Mary's Bill Chambers against Virginia on Feb. 14, 1953, an NCAA record.

$7,500 | Amount paid for rights to the first nationally televised title game, on NBC in 1954.

1980 | AN ALL-AMERICA trio of (from left) DePaul's Mark Aguirre, Virginia's Ralph Sampson and Maryland's Albert King rocked an All-American look. | *Photograph by* RAEANNE RUBINSTEIN

1986 | DAVID ROBINSON was braced for military service after the greatest hoops career in Navy history, leading the Midshipmen to the Elite Eight his junior year. | *Photograph by* BILL BALLENBERG

A TEAM THAT WAS BLESSED

BY FRANK DEFORD

Decades later, North Carolina's triple-overtime upset of Kansas and its goliath center Wilt Chamberlain in the 1957 title game still ranks as perhaps the greatest college basketball game ever played.   —*from* SI, MARCH 29, 1982

WHEN FRANK MCGUIRE left St. John's, in New York City, to become the coach at North Carolina in 1952, he had trouble persuading players to go South with him. This was because most of the best city players then were Roman Catholic, and the other coaches, friends and hangers-around, even a few priests, would tell a player and his parents that if the boy went with McGuire down to the Protestant Bible Belt, he would surely "lose his soul."

"This was my biggest hurdle—souls," McGuire says.

But he learned, to some extent, how to fight fire with fire. He would tell parents to look at it this way: Their boy wouldn't just be a basketball player, he'd also be serving as a missionary. And at some of the kitchen tables where McGuire raised this point, it went over very well.

The move South wasn't an easy transition for McGuire himself, either. He had come from the big time. The first game he coached at Chapel Hill, about 1,200 fans showed up in a gym that held only 5,632. His office was a shabby, reconstituted section of an old men's room, unable to accommodate two grown men standing shoulder to shoulder. The Carolina team traveled to away games in crowded private cars, and when the players arrived at the distant campus, they slept on cots set up in the host's gym.

For this bush stuff McGuire never would have left St. John's except for his son, Frankie. Frankie was retarded and had cerebral palsy, and it was very difficult caring for him in a small apartment in the big city. So it was that McGuire took little North Carolina up on its offer and then started to try to spirit the flower of high school basketball out of the archdiocese of New York.

It helped McGuire that a lot of the big city colleges recently had been caught fixing games; it also helped that Uncle Harry continued to work the territory for him. Uncle Harry was Harry Gotkin, his main talent scout back in the city.

Consequently, in their crew cuts and car coats, four defenders of the faith gathered as freshmen in Chapel Hill in the autumn of '54: Pete Brennan and Joe Quigg from Brooklyn, Bob Cunningham from West Harlem, and Tommy Kearns, who had grown up in the Bronx and moved across the river to Jersey, but commuted an hour and a half each way into Manhattan, to play for Looie Carnesecca at St. Ann's. Already at Chapel Hill, a year ahead of the other New Yorkers, was Lennie Rosenbluth, from the Bronx, a somewhat mysterious, wraithlike figure, 6' 5" and maybe 170, a Jew who didn't arrive at college until he was almost 20.

As Rosenbluth's senior season got underway, hopes were high that the Tar Heels would win the Atlantic Coast Conference, but Carolina dared harbor no serious aspirations of winning the national title, because everyone everywhere simply assumed that Kansas would win it in 1957. And in '58 and '59, for that matter. This was because a young giant from Philadelphia, Wilt Chamberlain, had decided to play for the Jayhawks, and now he was entering his sophomore year, his first of varsity eligibility.

He was then perceived as superhuman. "People today cannot imagine the impact that man had on us all at that time," Quigg says. "Wilt was just a colossus." He stood somewhat over seven feet, he was powerful and quick, and he was black! His reputation preceded him to Lawrence, Kans., because he was surely the first high school athlete whose recruiting was coast-to-coast news. The only question seriously debated was whether or not Wilt would destroy college basketball.

It didn't take long for teams that were playing Chamberlain to figure out that their only chance was to collapse the defense around him and hold the ball on offense. Kansas would even lose twice—both times by a basket in a low-scoring game on the road.

"Looking back, I don't ever remember feeling any pressure that season," Chamberlain says. "All I can remember is getting bored so often."

IT TOOK three overtimes, but the undersized Tar Heels finally subdued Chamberlain (with the ball) in the longest NCAA title game ever played.

MIDWAY THROUGH their schedule, with their record 16–0, North Carolina traveled to Maryland on a train and played the Terps before the largest basketball crowd in the history of the South, 12,200. When Maryland got possession of the ball, leading by four with 40 seconds left, McGuire called time out for the purpose of reviewing how the Tar Heels were to act—like gentlemen—in defeat. They won in overtime. "After that, after I called timeout to tell them how to lose, and still they couldn't, well, from then on I knew they were really something special," McGuire says.

The Tar Heels aligned themselves in such a way as to defy conventional defenses. "There was a chemistry, patterns, not plays," Rosenbluth says, "and when you have that, scouting reports don't mean a thing." In fact, broken down, the Carolina offense more closely resembled that used by the Harlem Globetrotters than any other. Rosenbluth was in the middle, back to the basket, the "showman," as the Globies call their "lead" (Meadowlark, Goose, Geese, whoever). Kearns was the "floorman" (Marques or Curly) out front with the ball. The two more traditional sturdy-center types, Quigg and Brennan, weren't under the basket, where they might get in the showman's way, but were put out in the corners.

Cunningham, at 6' 3", tall for a 1950s guard—and to gild the lily, McGuire listed him at 6' 4"—was the other starter. Just where were you, Bobby? "Sneakin'. Always sneakin' around," he says. "Lookin' after my children." He means the four more visible starters. Cunningham was the classic fifth man.

Carolina moved into the Final Four at 30–0. Unfortunately, if the Tar Heels got past Michigan State in the semis, their opponent in the championship game would surely be Kansas and Chamberlain, and they would have to face them in the Jayhawks' home territory, in Kansas City. As the Tar Heels' play-by-play announcer, Ray Reeve, was to say over the radio from K.C.: "Nobody's given them a Chinaman's chance."

Point of fact: Carolina had no business beating Michigan State. The Spartans' coach cried in the locker room afterward because he knew his team should have won. It took three overtimes and a lot of good luck, but the Tar Heels did win, and then they watched for a while as Chamberlain annihilated San Francisco in the other semi. Far from being intimidated, though, they came away calm in the knowledge of how they had to play him. "San Francisco let him get away with too much," Brennan says. "I don't care how awesome he was. We had to be physical with him." The next day, in the lobby of their hotel, the Continental, Kearns hung out, loving it, advising whatever skeptics would listen, "We're chilly. We're cool. Chamberlain won't give us any jitters." At some point, too (all accounts differ), McGuire told Kearns that if he was so cocky, he should go out and jump against Chamberlain at the start of the game. Kearns said sure.

AS THE FANS blinked and snickered, here came Kearns, 5' 10" and change, elbowing his way into the center circle opposite Chamberlain. The big man glared down. Kearns played it for all it was worth, tensing, getting way down as if he could spring 20 feet into the air.

So began the most exciting game in NCAA tournament history.

Carolina immediately assumed control. The Tar Heels collapsed two or three men on Wilt and dared the other Jayhawks to stick the ball in from outside. Kansas played a box-and-one, with Maurice King shadowing Rosenbluth. It was a disastrous strategy; it didn't contain Rosenbluth and it left the other Tar Heels free to shoot over the zone. Of the first seven shots they threw up, Brennan hit one, Rosenbluth, Kearns and Quigg two apiece. Twenty-five years later, Wilt still has the vision of the Carolina center, Quigg, staying way out, chewing gum, throwing up the jumper. It was 17–7 before the Jayhawks went to man-to-man and still 29–22 at the half.

Wilt led Kansas back, and before the second half was nine minutes gone, the Jayhawks were in front 36–35. Quigg and Rosenbluth were each to pick up his fourth foul along in here, too, but even when Chamberlain, then a fine free throw shooter, made both shots of a one-and-one to put Kansas up

COMING TO New York City for the '57 regionals was a homecoming for the Heels' (from left) Cunningham, Rosenbluth, Kearns, Quigg, Brennan and McGuire.

by three, Kansas coach Dick Harp kept the Jayhawks in a deliberate offense. Ironically, Harp still maintains, "Had a shot clock been employed then, no one would've been able to come even close to beating Wilt." But still, he elected to hold the ball.

It almost worked, too. Say that. With 1:45 left, Chamberlain, moving up high, whipped a beautiful pass down into Gene Elstun, who not only made the shot but also drew Rosenbluth's fifth foul. As Elstun stood at the line, it was 44–41, and Chamberlain distinctly recalls glancing up into the stands at this moment, spotting a good friend and sighing at him, at last sure of victory.

But Elstun missed, the Tar Heels scratched back, and in the waning seconds Kearns tied it at 46 from the line.

In the first overtime, each team scored only one basket; in the second, none. Back in North Carolina, it was chiming midnight as the Tar Heels went into a third overtime for the second straight night.

Kearns made a basket first and all of a one-and-one to put Carolina up four. But Wilt came back with a three-point play, and when King and Elstun sank free throws, Carolina had one shot, down 53–52. There were 10 seconds left when Quigg ended up with the ball near the top of the key. "It's funny," he says. "I rarely wanted the ball. But this night I'd felt good, right from the start." He made a slight pump fake and drove against the invincible Wilt Chamberlain himself. King, coming across to help out, fouled Quigg just as he got the shot off.

Before he walked to the free throw line, Quigg promised everybody that he would make them both. And he did. *Swish. Swish.* 54–53.

Not only that, but Quigg was also the one who batted away the last-ditch pass that was intended for Chamberlain in the low post. Kearns retrieved the ball with a couple seconds left, and after dribbling once, he heaved it away, high up in the air. It's so strange to see a game end that way, all the players looking straight up, half of them helplessly, half

in exultation. And then the clock runs out, and all the Kansas players drop their eyes to the floor and walk off. All the Carolina players suddenly lower their heads too—but not down, only around, finding one another, then running into each other's arms.

IN THOSE medieval times the championship was played in an arena lacking proper locker-room facilities, so the players dressed in their hotels. Quigg remembers the odd sensation of winning the national title and then "just running through the streets of Kansas City, all by myself." There was such a fuss made over the Tar Heels that the plane that brought them home the next day had to circle the Raleigh-Durham airport for some time until police could clear the runway of well-wishers.

Wilt Chamberlain left the arena in Kansas City for the lonely walk back to his hotel, the old Muehlebach. Against what was now a light rain, he wore a little British driving cap. A small boy from Chapel Hill, who had flown out for the games, ran in circles around the big man, cruelly taunting him, chanting, "We wilted the Stilt, we wilted the Stilt," over and over. But Chamberlain didn't take the bait. He only looked ahead and kept on walking.

In another hour or two he was back on campus in Lawrence. Louis Armstrong was playing there that evening. It was envisioned as a victory ball. "Old Satchmo was playing *When the Saints Go Marching In*, but we marched back losers instead," Chamberlain said ruefully a few weeks ago. As the years have passed he has come to understand how that one game in Kansas City changed the whole perception of him. He came in as the invincible giant, but when he went out, he carried with him some vague impression of defeat's being his destiny. It was with Bill Russell and the Celtics that this became a pox upon Chamberlain, but he knows only too well where the germ first alighted. He knows. "Of all the games in my career, and certainly so far as image is concerned, you understand, that goddam one against Carolina was the biggest," he says. . . .

AN EXHAUSTED but exuberant group of Tar Heels hoisted McGuire on their shoulders after toppling the Jayhawks in their own backyard, in Kansas City.

1985 | BOB KNIGHT set the tone at Indiana with three national crowns and some volatile outbursts, like his chair-tossing display against Purdue. | *Photograph by* ANGELA GOTTSCHALK

1981 | HURRYING HOOSIER Isiah Thomas blew by Carolina's Jimmy Black on the way to two of his game-high 23 points in Indiana's title-game victory. | *Photograph by* RICH CLARKSON

1989 | DIVISION II may be a step down in the NCAA, but the stakes were just as high for Southeast
Missouri State's Lawrence Wilson as his season ended in a title-game loss. | *Photograph by* CARL SKALAK

THE WHITTLER

BY GARY SMITH

Old school and colorful sometimes to a fault, Temple coach John Chaney used all his rage and passion to carve life's complexity down to a few simple certainties. —*from* SI, FEBRUARY 28, 1994

A MAN'S BORN INTO CRAZY. He's born into Black Bottom. That's low. That's lower than sea level. Shacks crouching in a hollow outside Jacksonville. A January baby, third year of the Depression. Every time it rains hard, the kitchen shed in the backyard fills and his mama cooks in brown water up to her arthritis. That's him, down there with the tadpoles and frogs. Lower than rat level.

He's born and he blinks and his father's gone. Nobody tells him that the next man's not his real daddy, but the boy gets this smoky feeling because the old man seems icier with him than with the boy's little brother and sister, and kids talk about how different he looks, and grown-ups' conversations end funny sometimes when he walks into a room. He calls his aunt "Mama" because she's the one who takes care of him while his mother works all day and half the night, cleaning up after white folks, later sewing garments in a sweatshop.

The family moves to Philadelphia when he's 14. He arrives, skinny as a finger, wearing long underwear and a tweed suit on a 95 degrees August day, and the city boys start laughing at him and his clothes and his drawl and his "Yes, sirs" and "No, ma'ams." He comes home one day and his aunt-mama's dead, leaving him to cook the family's dinner, rub the clothes across the washboard. Each day at his new junior high in South Philly, Dante and his boys stop him and demand the dime in his pocket, punch him in the gut, make him so scared that he gets headaches and skips his last class so he can race home before they set their ambush. So scared he's afraid to tell anyone; so scared he can't try out for basketball because that will give Dante the chance to corner him at the end of practice, alone, at dusk; so scared he hides on the fire escape to eat lunch. Until one day in wood-shop class, when John Chaney walks into the tool room and reaches for the mallet.

His players set their alarm clocks for 4:45 a.m., but sometimes fear awakens them a quarter hour early. Often they rise from dreams of their coach. They trudge through the cold darkness of North Philadelphia to the gym at five, change clothes, get taped and take the floor at 5:30.

John enters a little later. Limps in pigeon-toed, flat-footed, T-shirt hanging out, one pant leg halfway up his shin. "The beaten-down dog," says Paul Gibson, Temple's director of academic support for student athletes. "He enjoys being that."

The players gather around him. Oh, what a roll call he has had during his 10 years at Division II Cheyney State and a dozen more at Temple. McKinley Walker, with a bullet in his back and one blind eye; and Gerry Mills, placed in Chaney's custody by a judge for stealing a radio; and Eddie Geiger, a seven-foot dropout, working at a car wash, who had never played high school ball; and Frazier Johnson, whose mother was a junkie and whose father went out for a quart of milk one day and never came back; and Aaron McKie, whose dad died and whose mom left him; and Huey Futch, a freshman who was academically ineligible this season and who spent his last year of high school living alone in an apartment, cooking on a hot plate, under a roof half ripped off by Hurricane Andrew. Just thinking about them can make John cry. "Always leave the door open for a lost dog," his late mother, Earley, used to say.

He starts speaking to the players in that low, raspy voice and builds to an ear-blistering, ass-smoking, remove-the-women, hide-the-children, Sunday-Southern-preacher screech. His philosophy's the secretion of his life, fresh-squeezed, unstrained, pulp and seeds still in it. Everything dire: *Get BACK on defense! Your house's on FIRE, your MAMA and SISTER are in there BURNIN', get BACK!* Half of it hilarious, half cemetery serious, all of it raw. Might talk 10 minutes. Might talk an hour. Might talk four. Might talk Massachusetts' man defense. Might talk Mogadishu. Might talk Holocaust or haircuts—*No nubs! No naps! No EMBRYO HEADS!* Might jumble 'em all in a bag and spill 'em all out at once, somehow finding the connective truth that turns everything into analogy and allegory. "A message about life, every day," says La Salle coach Speedy Morris. "How many coaches give their kids that?"

He almost never plays his subs, even with a fat lead. Too scary. Never lets his players leave their areas of strength—*everybody in his room!* Never gives them four places to pass against a press, or three choices of defense. No, not the whittler. Gives them *one*. A poor boy's lesson, another Mama-ism: *You GOT to make it work when you only got one.*

And once he has them down to meat and bone, he holds them to the fire. . . .

NO NONSENSE barely begins to describe Chaney, who had 741 career wins and took Temple to the NCAA tournament 17 times in his 24 seasons there.

1961 | MEDFIELD COLLEGE gained a distinct height advantage when *The Absent-Minded Professor* equipped the players' shoes with Flubber. | *Photograph courtesy of* THE EVERETT COLLECTION

> Retrospective

Breaking Down The Film

Whether indicting the sport or celebrating it, movies have used the college game as a subject ever since Hank Luisetti was an All-America at Stanford— and then signed with Paramount to costar with Betty Grable in 1938's "Campus Confessions."

1951

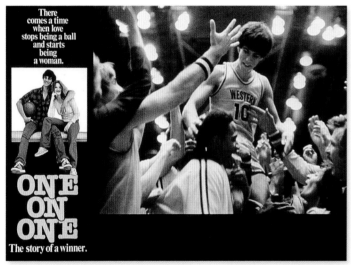

1977

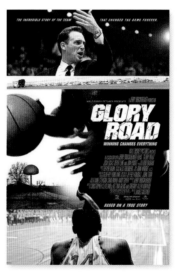

2006

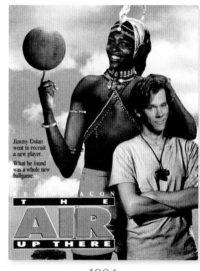

1994

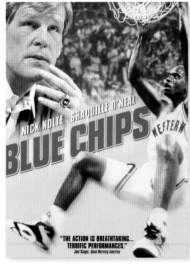

1994

1960

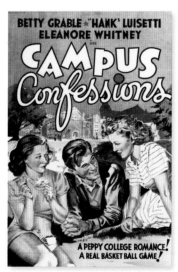

1938

1991 | GRANT HILL had Kansas's defenders back on their heels in the title game as Duke won for the first time after eight Final Four misses. | *Photograph by* JOHN W. MCDONOUGH

1984 | AKEEM OLAJUWON *reeled in a rebound for the Phi Slamma Jamma crew as Houston sent Memphis State packing in the Sweet 16.* | *Photograph by* RICHARD MACKSON

THE GREATEST UPSET NEVER SEEN

BY ALEXANDER WOLFF

On Dec. 23, 1982, with no TV cameras and very little press on hand, tiny Chaminade of Honolulu shocked Ralph Sampson and No. 1 Virginia, and college basketball hasn't been the same since.

—*from* SI, DECEMBER 31, 2007

MERV LOPES, 75 NOW, STILL wades into the Pacific off the Big Island of Hawaii to throw a cast net. He loves fishing for the sheer lottery of it, for never knowing exactly what he'll take in—yet he's as sure as the tides that he'll eventually catch the big one. "And after you catch the big one," he says, "you never stop talking about it."

A quarter century has passed since Chaminade, the NAIA school on a Honolulu hillside whose basketball team Lopes coached, found in its net the nation's No. 1 team, the undefeated Virginia Cavaliers of Ralph Sampson, the 7' 4" center who would be a three-time NCAA player of the year. Islanders and mainlanders alike still talk about what happened that night in the Neal Blaisdell Center, even if—or perhaps because—fewer than 4,000 people witnessed it. "It still gives you the chicken skin," says Lopes, using an Islandism for goose bumps. And it has given college basketball much more. The game helped usher in an era of upsets and parity, heralding the astonishing NCAA title won that spring by North Carolina State, and it assured that ESPN and its cable spawn would henceforth permit virtually no game to go untelevised.

Chaminade, with an enrollment of just 900 and run by the Marianists, paid Lopes only $10,000 a year to serve as coach, so he also held down a day job as a junior high guidance counselor. He begged towels from Waikiki Beach hotels. He drove the team's old Navy surplus van. He washed the players' uniforms himself. "Never complained once," he says, "because who the hell was gonna listen?"

Lopes's roster was every bit as jerry-built as his program. "The guys came from all different backgrounds and weren't too stable," Lopes says. "But they played hard and played together."

Forward Richard Haenisch, who had arrived in Hawaii from Frankfurt, Germany, as a 10th grader, enrolled at Chaminade because Lopes was the only coach to offer him a scholarship. Six-foot Tim Dunham, a preacher's son from Stockton, Calif., with a 42-inch vertical leap, "didn't drink and didn't smoke," Lopes recalls, "and didn't go to class too often."

Lopes found Dunham's backcourtmate, Mark Wells, playing pickup ball on L.A.'s Venice Beach. A former Chaminade player turned Lopes on to the lunch-bucket forward Ernest Pettway, then haunting a rec center in Pasadena. "He didn't shoot very well, but at least I didn't have to tell him not to," his coach recalls. Lopes landed another starter literally at home. Guard Mark Rodrigues was a distant relative of Lopes's.

Then, on the eve of the 1982–83 season, Lopes fielded a call from an Air Force enlisted man on Oahu. The airman told him he had a 6' 8" brother who was out visiting. Tony Randolph stood closer to 6' 6", but fatefully hailed from Staunton, Va., the town just down the Shenandoah Valley from Harrisonburg, where Ralph Sampson grew up. Randolph had guarded Sampson in high school and played rec ball against him dozens of times. He had even gone out with Ralph's sister Valerie.

Lopes asked Randolph to jump into a workout. After he threw down a dunk from the wing during a 3-on-2 drill, Lopes says, "We enrolled him, and that was it."

For Virginia's part, its date with Chaminade fell in the midst of a December designed as a kind of valedictory tour for the Cavaliers' senior center. On Dec. 11, at the Capital Centre in Landover, Md., Virginia defeated Georgetown and Hoyas sophomore Patrick Ewing in a made-for-Ted-Turner event hyped as the Game of the Decade. Sampson scored 23 points, grabbed 16 rebounds and blocked seven shots even though he was sick and "played because he kind of had to," remembers Jim Miller, who played at forward alongside Sampson.

Right afterward the Cavaliers were to fly to Tokyo, by way of New York City and Anchorage, to participate in the Suntory Ball, a three-team tournament sponsored by a Japanese distillery. But a blizzard delayed Virginia's departure. "By the time we got to Japan, we were basically hallucinating from sleep deprivation," remembers Virginia forward Tim Mullen.

Sampson was so dehydrated from an intestinal virus that he was hooked up to an IV in his hotel room, but Virginia

was deep enough to beat Phi Slamma Jamma without him, and then Utah, and landed in Honolulu 8–0.

Meanwhile, the Silverswords gave the Cavaliers little reason to fret. True, a week earlier they had beaten Hawaii, the state's lone Division I basketball school, for the first time ever. But two days before they were to face the Cavaliers, the Silverswords lost at home to Wayland Baptist, an NAIA team with a 5–9 record.

Television may have given the game a miss, but a videotape of remarkable quality, shot from the stands by a fan, has kicked around Chaminade for years. Watching it, one thing strikes you immediately: the confidence with which the Silverswords take the game to their guests. The shot clock would not be introduced for three more seasons, but Chaminade plays no stall ball and deploys no gimmicky defenses. Indeed, the Silverswords seem quicker than Virginia on the wings, and every bit

a match for the Cavaliers' backcourt of Othell Wilson and Rick Carlisle. As for Randolph, he has every reason to take his 7' 4" counterpart in stride. Ralph is just a country kid from down the valley. By the time Chaminade edges out to a 19–12 lead, Randolph has already begun feathering in jump shots from 17, 18, 19 feet—what will be nine all told in 12 attempts.

In the end Virginia has 25 turnovers, and combined with 39% shooting, that's enough to do in the Cavaliers. The final score: Chaminade 77, Virginia 72.

Haenisch sprints to one end of the court and, shinnying up by the basket brace and backboard, sits atop the rim. Someone hands him a pair of scissors, and soon he's brandishing the net, a giddy kid whose glee will be translated into the phrase that will grace T-shirts that all of UVA's rivals will covet: YES VIRGINIA, THERE IS A CHAMINADE. . . .

THE SILVERSWORDS ushered in an era of upsets with their stunning victory over Virginia as the 6' 6" Randolph (second from left) outscored the 7' 4" Sampson.

1962 | CHEERS TURNED to tears for Ohio State in Louisville's Freedom Hall as it met intrastate rival

Cincinnati in the NCAA final for the second straight year—and lost again. | *Photograph by* JOHN G. ZIMMERMAN

2010 | THE HUSKIES presented a formidable prospect to opponents with Maya Moore (23) in tow, winning 90 straight games in one stretch and two titles. | *Photograph by* BILL FRAKES

1957 | A STANDOUT in any lineup, Wilt Chamberlain made a particularly powerful impression at Kansas with his size and athleticism. | *Photograph by* RICH CLARKSON

COME SEE THE DINKA DUNKER DO

BY FRANZ LIDZ

International players have contributed greatly to the college game, none more entertainingly than a Sudanese tribesman by the name of Manute Bol. —*from* SI, DECEMBER 10, 1984

AS MORNING BROKE ON THE third day of his monthlong clinic with the Sudanese national basketball team in the summer of 1982, Fairleigh Dickinson coach Don Feeley stood on a scruff of hill in Khartoum and caught his first glimpse of Manute Bol. In the bright sun, Feeley watched Bol, all 7' 6" of him, loom over the outdoor court like a giant exclamation mark.

"Who's *that?*" Feeley asked the other Sudanese players.

"That's Manute," they all chorused.

"Boys," said Feeley after a long pause, "from now on we're going to play a very different game."

Traveling by train, it had taken Bol, a Dinka tribesman, six days to travel the 600 miles to Khartoum from his home village of Gogrial in the savanna country west of Sudan's vast, central swamp, the Sudd. Basketball was a relatively new game to Bol, who had been playing it for two years around Gogrial, but Feeley was struck by the way Bol could dunk while standing on his tiptoes and touch both sides of the backboard simultaneously. Probably because Bol distributed all that body on a mere 190-pound frame, Feeley's expectations for him were modest: "I thought of him more as the next Bill Russell than Wilt Chamberlain."

Feeley showed Bol which basket he should slam balls into and which basket to bat them away from. Now, Bol has it down pretty well. Since that fateful journey to Khartoum, he has followed the bouncing ball to Cleveland and Connecticut, where he's now a freshman at the University of Bridgeport. In his college debut on Nov. 19 he scored 20 points, had 20 rebounds and blocked six shots in a 75–63 victory over Stonehill College of North Easton, Mass. At the end of last week he was averaging 19.8 points, 16.5 rebounds and 8.5 blocks through four games, all of which Bridgeport had won.

Feeley returned from the Sudan, and after the 1982–83 season he was let go by Fairleigh Dickinson. So he steered Bol to Cleveland State, where Feeley's buddy, Kevin Mackey, was coach. But Bol didn't know how to read or write, which made it difficult for him to meet the NCAA's academic requirements. So Feeley sent him to nearby Case Western to learn English. Bol, obviously a fast learner, soon knew his new language well enough to understand that at Division I schools, the NCAA docks a player one year of eligibility for every year he is over the age of 20. Although Bol's passport indicates he's 21, some doubt its veracity. No wonder: The same document lists his height as 5' 2". Bol explains, "When they measured me, I was sitting down."

As a Division II team, Bridgeport isn't subject to the strict eligibility rules that Cleveland State is and Bol can play four years there. Not since that old showman P.T. Barnum discovered Charles Stratton, a.k.a. Tom Thumb, in Bridgeport in 1842 has a spectacle so astounded the local gentry. Bol dribbles down the floor on spindly, Q-tip legs, massaging the ball with long, sleek fingers. He has a watchful reserve and tends to show the same disdain for strangers that Dinka herdsmen display toward the 60 or so species of mosquitoes that inhabit the Sudd. "Getting Manute to give an interview," says coach Bruce Webster, "can be like pulling teeth." Which would not be easy with Bol, who is missing 15 choppers. He sacrificed four or five in a tribal ritual that marked his passage to manhood at age 14. And he lost a few more four years ago in his passage from backcourt to frontcourt. "The first stuff I ever try," he recalls, "the ball go *slam-dunk!* in the basket." And his front teeth went *bam thunk!* on the rim.

Bol got his first face job at 14. In a sort of Dinka Bar Mitzvah, an elder carved three lines across his forehead. The English translation of Manute is Only Son, and indeed he's the only son of Madot and Abouk Bol. (Ma Bol was 6' 10" and Pa Bol was 6' 8". Grandpa Bol Chol, chief of the Thwig tribe, is said to have been 7' 10", but he was born too early to be discovered by American hoop recruiters. Bol's sister, also named Abouk, who has never seen a basketball, is back home tending his 150 cattle. She's 6' 8".) But in Gogrial some of his friends still call him Raan Cheg. That's a Dinka joke. Raan Cheg means "short stuff." . . .

HE HAD just 190 pounds stretched over his 7' 6" frame, but the spindly Bol was a defensive stopper averaging 7.1 blocked shots a game as a freshman.

2008 | HOCUS-POCUS ON a shooter's focus was the aim of the Maryland crowd at the Comcast Center as it tried to distract Duke's DeMarcus Nelson at the free throw line. | *Photograph by* AL TIELEMANS

1950 | BOB COUSY brought his magical ballhandling from the streets of New York City
to Holy Cross, where he led the Crusaders to two Final Fours and a title. | *Photograph by AP*

1995 | STEVE NASH came almost unrecruited to Santa Clara from Canada and drove the Broncos to three NCAA tournament appearances. | *Photograph by* JOHN W. MCDONOUGH

THE
1960s

1964 | A PREPPY LOOK belied the beast in Bill Bradley, who led Princeton to its only Final Four, won Olympic gold as a junior and became a Rhodes Scholar.

Photograph by MARK KAUFFMAN

>> OFF TO SEE THE WIZARD

THE WORLD KEPT GETTING MORE MIXED up, and John Wooden kept instructing his UCLA boys on the correct way to lace up their sneakers. A motor-mouth named Cassius Clay beat Sonny Liston in February of 1964 and a month later Wooden won his first NCAA title. The first U.S. combat troops arrived in the distant jungles of Vietnam around the time that Wooden won his second, in 1965. Texas Western shocked the world in 1966, but Wooden was back the following year, winning a third title several months after *Hair* opened off-Broadway. Martin Luther King Jr. and Sen. Robert F. Kennedy were assassinated in 1968, the year that Wooden won his fourth.

A long-haired quarterback named Namath beat the Establishment in Super Bowl III; an X-rated *Midnight Cowboy* won the Academy Award; Charles Manson's gang did its butchery not five miles from Pauley Pavilion; and huge throngs made their way to concerts at Woodstock and Altamont, all in 1969. And in that year Wooden won again, turning back his alma mater, Purdue, in the title game.

Along the way, the Wizard of Westwood figured out how to communicate with a brooding philosopher (Lew Alcindor), who would be succeeded by a war-protesting free spirit (Bill Walton). And as he surveyed the fertile college basketball landscape of the late '60s, his gaze no doubt locked on LSU, where you could almost hear him saying to a floppy-haired kid named Maravich: "Goodness gracious sakes alive, Peter, pull up your socks and stop shooting so much!" —J.M.

Joe Cocker rocked Woodstock in '69.

> All-Decade Teams

FIRST TEAM

Walt Hazzard
G - UCLA

Pete Maravich
G - LSU

Bill Bradley
F - PRINCETON

Jerry Lucas
F - OHIO STATE

Lew Alcindor
C - UCLA

SECOND TEAM

Calvin Murphy
G - NIAGARA

Jimmy Walker
G - PROVIDENCE

Cazzie Russell
F - MICHIGAN

Elvin Hayes
F - HOUSTON

Wes Unseld
C - LOUISVILLE

NATIONAL CHAMPION

		COACH
'60*	OHIO STATE	Fred Taylor
'61	CINCINNATI	Ed Jucker
'62	CINCINNATI	Ed Jucker
'63	LOYOLA (ILL.)	George Ireland
'64	UCLA	John Wooden
'65	UCLA	John Wooden
'66	TEXAS WESTERN	Don Haskins
'67	UCLA	John Wooden
'68	UCLA	John Wooden
'69	UCLA	John Wooden

LEADING SCORER

	POINTS PER GAME
OSCAR ROBERTSON, Cincinnati	33.7
FRANK BURGESS, Gonzaga	32.4
BILLY McGILL, Utah	38.8
NICK WERKMAN, Seton Hall	29.5
HOWARD KOMIVES, Bowling Green	36.7
RICK BARRY, Miami	37.4
DAVE SCHELLHASE, Purdue	32.5
JIMMY WALKER, Providence	30.4
PETE MARAVICH, LSU	43.8
PETE MARAVICH, LSU	44.2

LEADING REBOUNDER

	REBOUNDS PER GAME
LEROY WRIGHT, Pacific	.234**
JERRY LUCAS, Ohio State	.198**
JERRY LUCAS, Ohio State	.211**
PAUL SILAS, Creighton	20.6
BOB PELKINGTON, Xavier	21.8
TOBY KIMBALL, Connecticut	21.0
JIM WARE, Oklahoma City	20.9
DICK CUNNINGHAM, Murray State	21.8
NEAL WALK, Florida	19.8
SPENCER HAYWOOD, Detroit	21.5

*DENOTES YEAR IN WHICH SEASON ENDED **LEADER DETERMINED BY PERCENTAGE OF BOTH TEAMS' REBOUNDS

>> WISH YOU WERE THERE

Cincinnati 70, Ohio State 65 (OT)

MARCH 25, 1961 • MUNICIPAL AUDITORIUM, KANSAS CITY, MO.

The Buckeyes have a chance to repeat as national champs but with one tick left in regulation Jerry Lucas's attempted tip-in of the inbounds pass goes off the rim. Forward Bob Wiesenhahn has 17 points and nine rebounds to lead the Bearcats to their first title.

Loyola 60, Cincinnati 58 (OT) >

MARCH 23, 1963 • FREEDOM HALL, LOUISVILLE

Led by star Jerry Harkness *(right),* Loyola rallies from 15 down to send the title game to OT and completes an improbable comeback when Vic Rouse scores the game-winning bucket on a put-back in the final second to end Cincinnati's hopes of becoming the first team to win three straight titles.

Princeton 118, Wichita State 82

MARCH 20, 1965 • MEMORIAL COLISEUM, PORTLAND

Bill Bradley punctuates one of the greatest individual performances in NCAA tournament history with 58 points in the national third-place game. That gives him a then-record total of 177 points for the tournament and Most Outstanding Player honors despite not even reaching the title game.

UCLA Freshmen 75, Varsity 60

NOVEMBER 27, 1965 • PAULEY PAVILION, LOS ANGELES

In the debut of Pauley Pavilion, freshmen Lew Alcindor, Lucius Allen, Lynn Shackelford and Co. give a preview of what lies ahead as they roll over the upperclassmen, who were then the defending national champions, in a highly publicized scrimmage. A crowd of 12,051 fills the new $5 million arena and sees Alcindor, the ballyhooed recruit from New York's Power Memorial High, score 31 points.

Houston 71, UCLA 69

JANUARY 20, 1968 • THE ASTRODOME, HOUSTON

Before a record crowd of 52,693 in the three-year-old Astrodome and a nationally syndicated TV audience at home, Elvin Hayes scores 39 points to give the No. 2 Cougars a win and end the No. 1 Bruins' win streak at 47. Lew Alcindor, hampered by an eye injury, scores just 15 points on 4-of-18 shooting.

GAME CHANGER
JOHN WOODEN
THE 2-2-1 ZONE PRESS

Scourge of a generation, UCLA's vaunted zone-press defense makes the backcourt into a minefield for opposing ball handlers. To blunt an opponent's attack at its start and create turnovers, the two guards on defense *(1 and 2 in blue in all three diagrams)* relentlessly pressure (and often double-team) the opposing players in the backcourt. The forwards *(3 and 4 in blue)* are positioned to prevent a straight pass upcourt. The center *(not shown)* plays free safety.

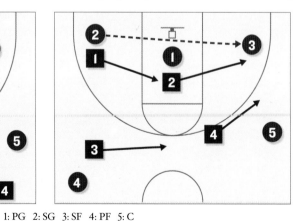
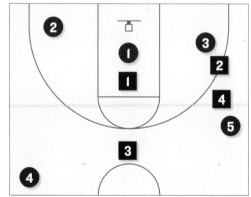

PASS ----------> CUT ———→ 1: PG 2: SG 3: SF 4: PF 5: C

>> TIME CAPSULE

THE MAN Off the court, LSU's Pete Maravich didn't look like a player—let alone the greatest scorer in college history. But with the rock in his hands Pistol Pete was a magician. It no doubt helped that his father, Press, was the coach, but given free rein, Pete made the most of it, with Globetrotters-quality showmanship and deft shooting from anywhere on the floor to the tune of 44.2 points a game for his career, a record that will likely stand forever.

THE WOMAN In a time of unlimited eligibility, Doris Rogers won an AAU championship in each of her eight seasons at the Nashville Business College (1962–69), and was an All-America seven times. Known as much for her blonde bouffant as her deadly two-handed set shot, the Bomber, as she was known, was a member of the 1964 U.S. World Championship team in Lima, Peru, where she represented the squad in the event's beauty pageant. She placed second.

THE STREAK From Dec. 5, 1962 through Feb. 22, 1964, North Carolina's Billy Cunningham scored at least 10 points and grabbed at least 10 rebounds in every game he played, a span of 40 straight—the longest streak of Division I double doubles either before or since.

THE CINDERELLA At a time when blacks weren't allowed to play at many Southern schools, Texas Western started five African-Americans. Often dismissed as undisciplined despite a 23–1 regular-season record and No. 2 ranking in 1965–66, the Miners shocked the world and struck a significant blow for racial equality when they ran the table in the NCAA tournament, beating Cincinnati and Kansas in overtime, then Utah, and finally Kentucky, from the all-white SEC, which they topped 72–65 in the title game in College Park, Md., not far from the Mason-Dixon line.

Houston's cheerers were ID'd by name in '68.

BASKETBALL BABYLON
UCLA'S DARK SECRET

The UCLA dynasty always seemed beyond reproach but behind the scenes a millionaire alum named Sam Gilbert *(left)* was supplying players with free or deeply discounted cars, stereos, airplane tickets and even abortions for players' girlfriends, according to a 1981 *Los Angeles Times* investigation. "If a ball player impregnated someone there was always a hospital available," former Bruins star Lucius Allen told the *Times.* An NCAA investigation resulted in a relative slap on the wrist for UCLA. The school was told to distance itself from Gilbert, who until his death in 1987 vehemently denied any wrongdoing, especially the abortion allegations.

> BY THE NUMBERS

10 Seasons, from 1967 until '76, that the so-called Lew Alcindor Rule was in effect, banning the slam dunk.

1,329 Points scored by Winston-Salem State's Earl Monroe in 1966–67, still a Division II single-season record. (Only D-I's Pete Maravich, with 1,381 in '69–70, had more.)

16 Consecutive field goals made by Kent State's Doug Grayson in a 107–83 loss to North Carolina on Dec. 6, 1967, a D-I record.

1 Heisman Trophy winner, Oregon State's Terry Baker, ever to play in a Final Four, in '63.

1 Number of games Detroit's Spencer Haywood was suspended for throwing a punch at a ref on Feb. 12, 1969.

8 Career 50-point performances by Miami's Rick Barry, the only man ever to win scoring titles in the NCAA, ABA and NBA.

6 Years ('63–68) syndicated Sports Network broadcast NCAA championship games, for total of $140,000.

2005 | KEITH LANGFORD (5) of Kansas defends his home court and its logo of the
Jayhawk, which has been part of the Rock Chalk cheer since 1886. | *Photograph by* GREG NELSON

A Star In the Making

Awkward, shy and terribly nearsighted, 6'10" George Mikan lacked the neccesary specs for greatness at DePaul, but constant drilling and dogged determination made him a player who would forever change the game and earn him the nickname Mr. Basketball

1945 | MIKAN, WITH COACH RAY MEYER

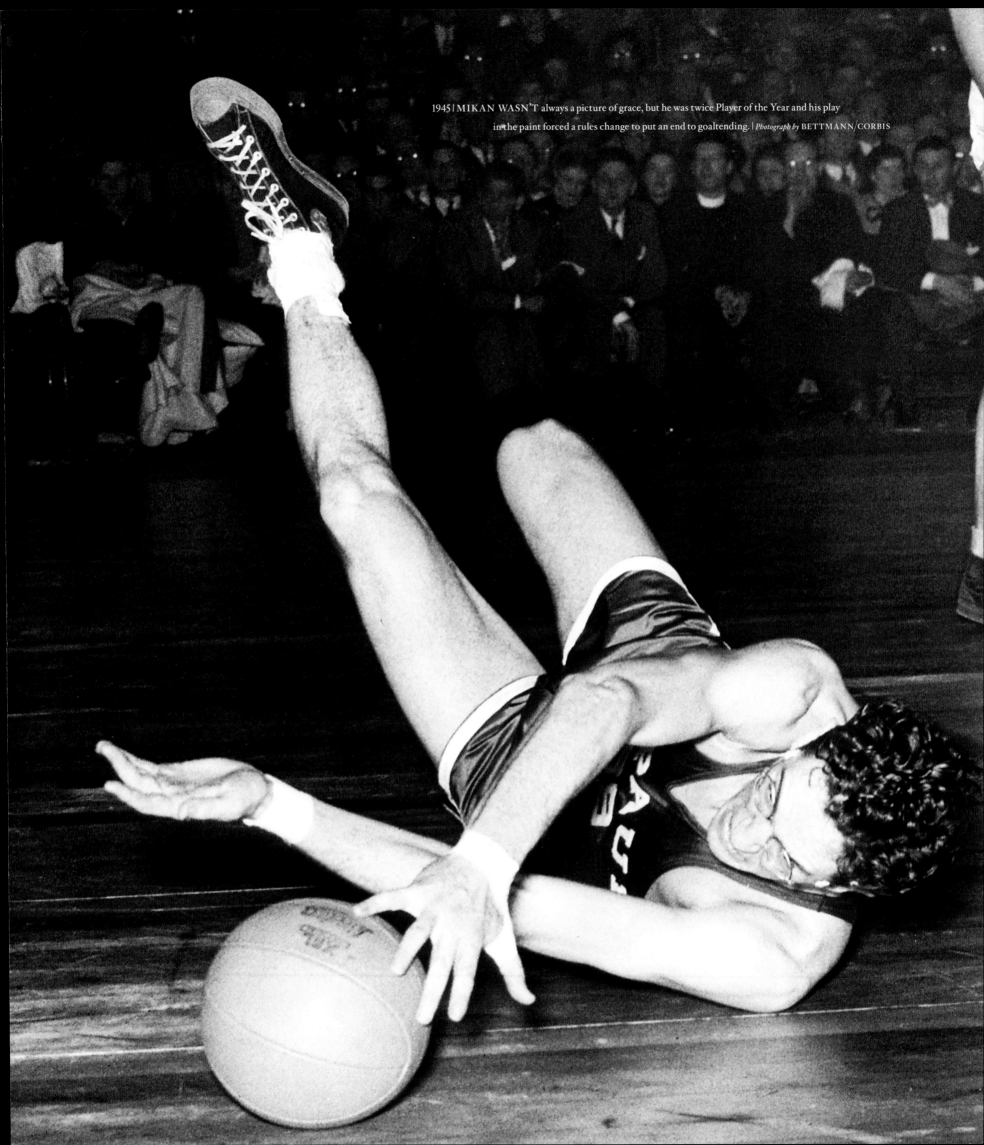

1945 | MIKAN WASN'T always a picture of grace, but he was twice Player of the Year and his play in the paint forced a rules change to put an end to goaltending. | *Photograph by* BETTMANN/CORBIS

GHOSTS OF MISSISSIPPI

BY ALEXANDER WOLFF

Even as late as 1963, segregationist policies barred some Southern teams from competing against black players—until one courageous Mississippi State team took a stand in the NCAA tournament.

—*from* SI, MARCH 10, 2003

THIS IS ULTIMATELY A STORY of how useful a basketball court can be. It does not, however, begin on a court, but over one, in the rafters of Humphrey Coliseum on the campus of Mississippi State in Starkville. There banners testify to how the Maroons, as they were then known, once interrupted Kentucky's basketball dominance in the Southeastern Conference with four SEC titles in five years, beginning with the 1958–59 group on which Bailey Howell starred as a senior. But there's a fifth banner that hangs near the four from the SEC; it reads NCAA TOURNAMENT 1963. No NCAA tournament banner hangs for the '62 SEC champions, or the '61 champs, either, or for the '59 Maroons. There's an explanation for their absence, a story that's painful for Howell to recall.

In December 1956, during Howell's sophomore season, the Maroons had beaten Denver in the opening round of a holiday tournament in Evansville, Ind. When word got back to Starkville that the Pioneers had fielded two black players and that the University of Evansville, which the Maroons were set to play for the title, would suit one up, school president Ben Hilbun and athletic director C.R. (Dudy) Noble summoned their all-white team home. That was the policy of the rearguard Board of Trustees for State Institutions of Higher Learning, which was packed with appointees of a long line of segregationist governors.

Two seasons later, in March 1959, the players hoped the school might ignore the policy that Mississippians widely accepted as unwritten law and let the Maroons build on their SEC title. Instead, second-place Kentucky represented the conference in the NCAAs. "It was a bitter disappointment," Howell says today. "But back then you didn't make waves." With members of the state's white power structure pledged to defend racial segregation against all comers, no trifling tournament was going to prod the team onto a court with Negroes.

So matters stood in February 1963. Five months earlier,

two people had been shot and killed amid a cloud of tear gas and gunsmoke in Oxford when federal marshals, who were sent there to uphold the right of a black man, James Meredith, to enroll at the University of Mississippi, clashed with segregationist demonstrators. More than 30 Mississippi State students had taken part in the segregationist riot at Ole Miss, and 15 were arrested. But now thousands of students, and pockets of influential alumni, began to urge school president Dean W. Colvard to send the team to the NCAAs if the Maroons went on to win their third straight SEC title, which they seemed poised to do.

On March 2, Colvard released a statement: The school would send its team "unless hindered by competent authority." The announcement touched off a dozen days of controversy, suspense and intrigue, concluded by the team's literally sneaking out of Starkville for the NCAA Mideast Regional in East Lansing, Mich. There the Maroons would face Loyola of Chicago, the eventual national champion, which had four black starters.

The race issue had hung over Loyola's season every bit as much as it had Mississippi State's. The Ramblers could hardly avoid it, not during an era when most coaches outside the South didn't dare play more than one black at home and two on the road. In a game at Houston, fans chanted, "Our team is red-hot, your team is all black," and as the Ramblers left the floor at halftime, spectators spat and threw coins.

The meeting with Mississippi State might have been the mother of all such grudge matches. But in the run-up to the game, the Loyola players felt a welter of emotions. "We got letters from the Klan," remembers Jerry Harkness, the Loyola captain. "At the same time we were getting pressure from the black community: 'You can't lose this game!' And there we were, in the middle."

Meanwhile, as they awaited the arrival of the Maroons— the word *maroon*, ironically, was an old Southern term for a runaway slave—the Ramblers couldn't help but admire them. "After we heard what they'd done to get there, all of us had our hats off to them," Harkness says.

Only just before tip-off, when he came out to shake hands with Mississippi State forward Joe Dan Gold, did Harkness realize what he would be a party to: "That's when I first felt that this was more than a basketball game. I couldn't believe how many flashbulbs went off, when all I'd done was shake his hand." . . .

THE HANDSHAKE between Gold (far right) and Harkness before the Ramblers' 61–51 victory was a historic moment signaling the decline of segregation in sports.

2006 | BROBDINGNAGIAN BUCKEYE Greg Oden was king of the court in his lone season in Columbus, as he led Ohio State to the national title game. | *Photograph by* JOE MCNALLY

1997 | AT A MERE 5' 5", Eastern Michigan's Earl Boykins could look small next to a ball, but he was third in the nation in scoring as a senior, at 25.7 points a game. | *Photograph by* PETER READ MILLER

1956 | DAYTON SEVEN-FOOTER Bill Uhl, a second-team All-America, was a Flyer at his apex as he let go of a hook shot against Iona. | *Photograph by* HY PESKIN

1970 | THE A-TRAIN, Artis Gilmore, took Jacksonville all the way to the title game with his suffocating D on St. Bonaventure in the semis. | *Photograph by* RICH CLARKSON

A DANDY IN THE DOME

BY JOE JARES

It was a titanic matchup—Lew Alcindor vs. Elvin Hayes—in a fittingly spectacular setting: the recently opened Houston Astrodome. It also gave TV execs the first inkling that college hoops could be a good business. —*from* SI, JANUARY 29, 1968

WHEN UCLA RECRUITED Lew Alcindor and a courtload of other skilled basketball players, it was generally assumed that the Bruins would shoot and rebound and full-court-press their way to a hundred or so consecutive victories. Easy. The Alcindor-led group, to nobody's surprise, went unbeaten as freshmen and once even mangled the varsity by 15 points. Packing their new campus arena as sophomores (with junior Mike Warren added), they ran through 30 victories to a national title, and this season they upped that streak to 47—until last Saturday night, when the dream of perfection was ruined.

At least UCLA lost in style. Before the largest crowd ever to see a basketball game in the U.S. (52,693), in Houston's famous Astrodome and before the biggest television audience in the history of the sport (150 stations in 49 states), Houston's Big E, 6' 8" senior Elvin Hayes, hit 68% of his shots, scored 39 points, took down 15 rebounds and made the two deciding free throws to beat the Bruins 71–69.

UCLA was ranked first in both wire-service polls; Houston was ranked second and had won 48 straight games at home. The Cougars had won 17 in a row since losing to UCLA in last year's NCAA semifinal, and Hayes was the third leading scorer in the nation and certainly no stranger. The city of Houston was all atwitter about the confrontation, to the point that one radio station kept listeners up to date with "KTHT Ruin-the-Bruins time is five-oh-four." The manager of UCLA's motel provided a 10-foot bed with BIG LEW printed in large letters at the foot.

By mid-December, 40,000 tickets had already been sold by mail and more than 150 had been given away to promising high school football players—just to prove that Texans still love football best. "I've had calls from people all over the country wanting to fly in for the game," said Dome ticket manager Dick McDowell. "We've had calls from Mexico City, Chicago and San Francisco. If we hadn't run out we would have sold 75,000 tickets, no doubt about it."

The best preparation Houston coach Guy V. Lewis could make was to keep the Big E healthy, and he knew it. But just in case Elvin wasn't going to be enough, Guy V. took some other precautions, like working diligently against a full-court press and being sure not to wear the pink-and-white-checked sport coat he wore against the Bruins in the NCAA loss. He wore a turquoise-and-black-checked jacket instead. All season at home games Houston had sat on the left side of the scorer, and that's how the Astrodome seating plan was made. Then Guy V. remembered the Cougars had sat on the left side in the NCAA loss, and he made his sports publicist switch the seating. UCLA sat on the left Saturday night and also was brought into the Astrodome through gate 13 for its Friday workout.

But no superstitious gimmicks were really needed. Hayes completely outplayed Alcindor, though it should be noted that Lew had suffered a scratched left eyeball in a previous game against Cal. Alcindor did not play in subsequent wins over Stanford and Portland. He wore an eyepatch and stayed in bed part of the week, and the inactivity no doubt affected his play. He made only four of 18 shots in one of the least impressive performances in his college career, a shame because it came before an audience that stretched, through TV cables anyway, to Fairbanks, Alaska.

What a scene it was. There were three bands, with two sets of pompon girls anxious to dance to every number. There was a student dressed up like a bruin, another dressed like a female bruin, another dressed like a cougar and then a real-live cougar named Shasta. There were writers from Cocoa, Fla., Pittsburgh, Mexico City and Conroe, Texas. The U.S. Information Agency was there to film a five-minute TV show to be seen in 33 countries.

If the atmosphere was carnival, it was just right for Judge Roy Hofheinz, the majordomo of the Dome and the man who owns Ringling Bros.-Barnum & Bailey Circus. Why, when the judge first thought of basketball in the Astrodome, he envisioned three games going on at once. The judge wants to host an NCAA tournament soon, and there was an NCAA committee on hand Saturday to watch the proceedings. Hopefully, the members will report that, while the Dome is an exciting and lucrative place, basketball is not a game to be watched through binoculars. . . .

THE ASTRODOME was the only venue big enough for the monumental game that pitted Elvin Hayes and No. 2 Houston against Lew Alcindor and No. 1 UCLA.

2007 | M-BLAZONED WITH the Wolverines' football-helmet design, Brent Petway showed his pride in Michigan before a game with rival Ohio State. | *Photograph by* REBECCA COOK

1976 | DAVE CORZINE (40) and Curtis Watkins of DePaul outposition and out-'do VMI's Ron Carter on the glass in the second round of the NCAAs. | *Photograph by* NEIL LEIFER

From Hardwood to Diamonds

Before they made it to the big leagues, a number of notable baseball stars had a short-pants romance with college basketball, demonstrating a superior all-around athleticism that would serve them well later

1939 | JACKIE ROBINSON
UCLA

1956 | BOB GIBSON
CREIGHTON

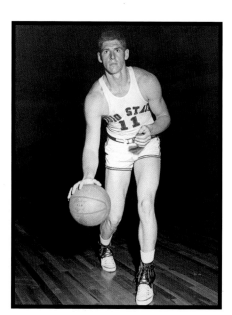

1957 | FRANK HOWARD
OHIO STATE

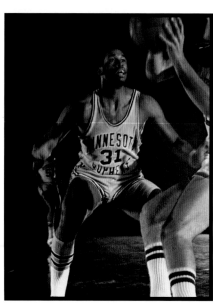

1973 | DAVE WINFIELD
MINNESOTA

1980 | TONY GWYNN
SAN DIEGO STATE

1999 | CHRIS YOUNG
PRINCETON

1951 | DICK GROAT, an All-America guard at Duke, scored a then single-season NCAA record of 831 points before becoming an MVP shortstop in Pittsburgh. | *Photograph by* KAUFFMAN/WALKER

1991 | THE FAB FIVE of (from far left) Jalen Rose, Juwan Howard, Jimmy King, Chris Webber and Ray Jackson (with coach Steve Fisher) made an indelible mark at

Michigan, but it didn't end well when Webber's TO earned a T and cost the Wolverines a shot at a win in the '93 title game. | *Photographs by* JODI BUREN *(left) and* JOE DEVERA

HOME ON THE RANGE

BY STEVE RUSHIN

Perhaps no player in the history of the college game improved from his first day on campus to his last as much as Bryant Reeves, who came to Oklahoma State from a small town and left renowned far and wide, as Big Country. —*from SI, NOVEMBER 29, 1993*

HIS PANTS CAME FROM A Big & Tall catalog. So did his dreams. The pants could be delivered in six to eight weeks, but the impossibly large dreams took longer to find him. A dream could pass through Gans, Okla., (pop. 346) without ever knowing it had been there. How did Bryant (Big Country) Reeves describe his hometown? "There's a schoolhouse," he said. "Drive a little further and there's a post office. Drive a little further and you're out of town."

His dreams were too big for his oversized britches. Reeves became convinced of this in the hours before his second college basketball game at Oklahoma State—against Purdue in the preseason NIT two years ago. Big Country paced a country mile in the Cowboys locker room. When his coach, Eddie Sutton, told him not to be nervous, Reeves replied, "I'm not nervous about the game, Coach. But when we beat Purdue, we have to fly to New York City, and I've never been on an airplane before."

Before Big Country saw the Big Apple as a freshman, before he became the Big Eight Player of the Year as a sophomore last season, before he toured Europe with a team of All-Americas this past summer, the farthest he had strayed from Gans was a recruiting visit to Creighton University. Omaha may as well have been Beijing to this small-town boy from a high school graduating class of 15. What was it Reeves said when he was still a Gans Grizzly, when Oklahoma State assistant Bill Self informed the recruit that he had to play in the city to improve his game?

"I've *been* playing in the city," said Big Country.

"Oklahoma City?" asked Self, now the head coach at Oral Roberts. "Or Tulsa?"

Quoth Country, "Sallisaw."

There are but 7,122 stories in the naked city of Sallisaw, Okla. Imagine Big Country's astonishment, then, when he flew to New York that November night two years ago. As the twinkling skyline of the great metropolis suddenly appeared beneath the airplane, Big Country whispered, "It sure is big." The plane was over Tulsa.

Big Country is 84 inches of snuff-dipping center who equaled another Dipper last season when he became the first player since Wilt Chamberlain of Kansas in 1958 to lead their conference in scoring (19.5 points per game), rebounding (10.0) and field goal percentage (62.1). His legend was secured last Feb. 24, in a home court win over Missouri. With two seconds left and the Cowboys inbounding from their own baseline and trailing by three, Country caught a long pass at halfcourt, spun, shot and immediately threw up his arms in the signal for a successful three-point field goal. A second later the ball hit the backboard and ripped through the hoop at the horn. "When it left my hands, it felt good," Country explains.

The original plan at Oklahoma State was to redshirt Big Country as a freshman. When Reeves arrived in Stillwater, he reluctantly removed his T-shirt for Cowboys strength coach Leroy Youster, triggering a frightening flabalanche that caught Youster by surprise. "God a'mighty, Coach," he said to Sutton. "What do you want me to do with *this*?"

"I grabbed Country's arm," recalls Youster, fixing a grip on your biceps. "It was like grabbing an old lady's arm. You know, a lot of . . . *mush and bone*."

The strength coach surveys the State weight room, a gleaming gift from former Cowboys javelin thrower Garth Brooks, and recalls Country's first workout there. "He was using 15-pound dumbbells, and his arms were all over the place," says Youster. "I'm trying to monitor him, but I don't have an eight-foot wingspan."

Suddenly, the strength coach himself goes soft—all mush, no bone. "I wish everyone worked as hard as he does," says Youster. "He'd go back to his dorm and throw up every night. Now, he uses 85-pound dumbbells; his arms are firm. In 11 years of doing this, I've never seen anybody improve as much as he has."

At Reeves's first practice in Gallagher-Iba Arena, the legendary coach Henry Iba sat watching from the sidelines and turned to Sutton. "Ed," said Iba. "That boy has a long way to go."

"A week later, he'd made amazing progress," says Sutton, who has framed basketball cards in his office of 14 of his players who made it to the NBA. "I've had a lot of nice players, but I've never had one develop as quickly as Country." . . .

REEVES CAME unpolished from rural Oklahoma and by his sophomore year had broken from the herd to lead the Big Eight in scoring and rebounding.

1982 | RALPH SAMPSON couldn't get the upper hand in this rebounding battle with Patrick Ewing, but Virginia did win the war, 68–63. | *Photograph by* MANNY MILLAN

1968 | A VENGEFUL Lew Alcindor gave Elvin Hayes (44) the hook as UCLA routed Houston to make up for an earlier defeat in the Astrodome. | *Photograph by* RICH CLARKSON

2001 | HAMPTON COACH Steve Merfeld got a huge lift from his 15th-seeded Pirates as they celebrated their shocking first-round upset of Iowa State. | *Photograph by* ROBERT BECK

1981 | STORMIN' MORMON Danny Ainge of BYU was exultant after driving the length of the court with :08 left to beat Notre Dame in the NCAAs. | *Photograph by* MANNY MILLAN

A TEAM ON A MISSION

BY SHELLEY SMITH

Hank Gathers is one of only three players ever to lead the nation in scoring and rebounding in the same season, averaging 32.7 points and 13.7 boards a game in 1988–89. Perhaps that made it all the more shocking when he collapsed and died during a game a week before the 1990 NCAA tournament. —from SI, MARCH 26, 1990

THE FIRST FULL PRACTICE came two days after a campus memorial service for their friend and teammate. Yet even with the finality of that ceremony, Loyola Marymount's basketball players found it hard to remember that Hank Gathers was really gone.

As the team formed a circle for its stretching exercises on March 8, forwards Per Stumer and Chris Scott unconsciously left a space for Gathers between them. When the drills began, Stumer stood motionless at midcourt, momentarily confused. For two years, he and Gathers had drilled together; now Stumer had no partner. Backup center Chris Knight, who had long coveted a starting role, began to shake when he was told to take Gathers's spot. "I felt guilty," says Knight. "Like I had something to do with his death."

It was only four days earlier that Gathers had collapsed and died of heart failure during a West Coast Conference tournament game against Portland on Loyola's home floor in Los Angeles. "We had a lot to deal with quickly," says Loyola forward Bo Kimble, who had been a friend of Gathers's for the past 10 years. "It was hard on everyone. But we knew Hank would have wanted us to play in the NCAAs. At the memorial service [in Loyola's Gersten Pavilion] I looked over and saw his coffin was in the paint. I knew then we would have to find a way to win for him."

And, perhaps astonishingly, they did. Playing in the West Regional in Long Beach, Calif., the 11th-seeded Lions beat No. 6–seed New Mexico State last Friday 111–92. Kimble scored 45 points and grabbed 18 rebounds, despite playing the entire second half with four fouls. On Sunday, Loyola crushed defending national champion Michigan 149–115 to shatter the tournament record for most points scored by a team (the previous mark was held by St. Joseph's, which got 127 in a four-overtime game against Utah in 1961) and earn a berth against Alabama in the West Regional semifinals,

in Oakland. Leading the Lions were Jeff Fryer, who poured in 41 points, including 11 of 15 shots from three-point range; Kimble, who added 37 points; and guard Terrell Lowery, who had 23.

Nobody made a motivational speech at either game. Nobody had to. Coach Paul Westhead's biggest concern was that his team would play with too much emotion, that it would equate caring about Gathers with winning. "Our feelings about Hank Gathers are irrelevant to whether we make a jump shot or not," he told the Lions early last week. "If we lose, it's not because we didn't care enough."

At a team meeting, Kimble encouraged his teammates to loosen up. Staying loose was something Gathers had insisted on. Even after a defeat, he would try to make his teammates feel better by kidding them until they couldn't help but smile. "If Hank saw us sitting around feeling sad, crying, he'd laugh his heart off at us," says Kimble. "I decided that Hank wasn't going to laugh at me."

To be sure, Kimble had his down moments last week. He didn't sleep for three days after Gathers died, and he began to realize that he was placing too much pressure on himself with his vow to make "something happen" every time he touched the ball. But he stuck to his promise to shoot his first free throw in every game lefthanded, in honor of Gathers, who had struggled so much with his foul shots this season that he had taken to shooting them lefty. "It may sound corny," says Kimble, who leads the nation in scoring with a 35.7 average, "but it makes me believe I've got a little bit of Hank inside me. I feel his strength."

Kimble's first lefthanded attempt didn't come until the second half of the New Mexico State game. Loyola had just blitzed the Aggies with an 18–4 spurt to start the half when Kimble was fouled in the act of shooting. As he approached the line, the partisan crowd, many wearing HANK armbands, began to buzz and then went quiet. Kimble shook his left arm, took the ball from the official and calmly made the shot. His teammates and coaches leaped in the air, many of them near tears.

"Playing the game, we didn't forget about Hank, but we were concentrating so much we weren't really thinking about him," said reserve guard Greg Walker. "When Bo got up there and shot lefthanded, it just brought back the whole reason why we're here, why we're playing." . . .

A MOURNING Kimble shot his first free throw lefthanded in tribute to his friend Gathers as the Lions shocked the field with an Elite Eight finish in 1990.

1992 | JASON KIDD lay between the rock and a hard place at Cal, where the Bay Area native led a basketball rebirth in the '90s. | *Photograph by* ANDY FREEBERG

2007 | CANDACE PARKER developed an iron will for winning at Tennessee, leading the Lady Vols to two straight NCAA championships. | *Photograph by* CLAY PATRICK McBRIDE

1960 | PAUL HOGUE (22) came up short against Cal in this Final Four, but he'd rebound to lead Cincinnati to national crowns the next two seasons. | *Photograph by* JON BRENNEIS

1966 | TEXAS WESTERN'S Harry Flournoy (44) beat Pat Riley to the ball as the Miners' all-black starters topped all-white Kentucky's for a historic title. | *Photograph by* JAMES DRAKE

THE
1970s

1971 | TOM McMILLEN (left) and Len Elmore
brought attitude, aptitude and—at 6' 11" and 6' 9",
respectively—altitude to Maryland, which went 73–17
in their three varsity seasons at College Park.
Photograph by JAMES DRAKE

>> THE FORCE BE WITH YOU

IN MARCH OF 1972 CONGRESS SENT THE EQUAL Rights Amendment to the states for ratification, around the time that Immaculata was winning the first of its three consecutive titles in the AIAW tournament, the predecessor to the women's NCAAs. A few years later, even male hoops fans began to notice a UCLA phenom named Ann Meyers, who became the first player of either gender to register a quadruple double.

Change was everywhere. By 1971 *Doonesbury* and *All in the Family* were challenging the conventions of the comic strip and the small screen; by 1975 Bill Gates had started Microsoft; and in 1979 Margaret Thatcher became prime minister of Great Britain.

In that spirit, the men's NCAA tournament could hardly have stood still. The tipping point for expansion came in 1974 when Maryland, the No. 4–ranked team in the country with six future draft choices, was not invited to the NCAA dance, the consequence of its memorable 103–100 overtime loss to N.C. State in the ACC tournament final. The following year the NCAA tournament field was expanded from 25 to 32.

But that was only the beginning. *Star Wars* was released in 1977, two years before the college hoops version came out—the epic NCAA title-game battle in which Magic Johnson faced off against Larry Bird. The game got such boffo reviews that the following year the tournament field was increased from 40 to 48 . . . and it was onward and upward from there. —J.M.

Luke, Leia and Han Solo exploded in popular culture in '77.

> All-Decade Teams

FIRST TEAM

Phil Ford
G - NORTH CAROLINA

Earvin (Magic) Johnson
G - MICHIGAN STATE

Larry Bird
F - INDIANA STATE

David Thompson
F - NORTH CAROLINA STATE

Bill Walton
C - UCLA

SECOND TEAM

Darrell Griffith
G - LOUISVILLE

John Lucas
G - MARYLAND

Scott May
F - INDIANA

Marques Johnson
F - UCLA

Kent Benson
C - INDIANA

NATIONAL CHAMPION

		COACH
'70*	UCLA	John Wooden
'71	UCLA	John Wooden
'72	UCLA	John Wooden
'73	UCLA	John Wooden
'74	NORTH CAROLINA STATE	Norm Sloan
'75	UCLA	John Wooden
'76	INDIANA	Bob Knight
'77	MARQUETTE	Al McGuire
'78	KENTUCKY	Joe B. Hall
'79	MICHIGAN STATE	Jud Heathcote

*DENOTES YEAR IN WHICH SEASON ENDED

LEADING SCORER

	POINTS PER GAME
PETE MARAVICH, LSU	44.5
JOHNNY NEUMANN, Mississippi	40.1
DWIGHT (BO) LAMAR, Southwestern Louisiana	36.3
WILLIAM (BIRD) AVERITT, Pepperdine	33.9
LARRY FOGLE, Canisius	33.4
BOB McCURDY, Richmond	32.9
MARSHALL ROGERS, Texas-Pan American	36.8
FREEMAN WILLIAMS, Portland State	38.8
FREEMAN WILLIAMS, Portland State	35.9
LAWRENCE BUTLER, Idaho State	30.1

LEADING REBOUNDER

	REBOUNDS PER GAME
ARTIS GILMORE, Jacksonville	22.2
ARTIS GILMORE, Jacksonville	23.2
KERMIT WASHINGTON, American	19.8
KERMIT WASHINGTON, American	20.4
MARVIN BARNES, Providence	18.7
JOHN IRVING, Hofstra	15.4
SAM PELLOM, Buffalo	16.2
GLENN MOSLEY, Seton Hall	16.3
KEN WILLIAMS, North Texas	14.7
MONTI DAVIS, Tennessee State	16.2

>> WISH YOU WERE THERE

UCLA 87, Memphis State 66

MARCH 26, 1973 • ST. LOUIS ARENA, ST. LOUIS In the most dominant performance in NCAA tournament history, Bill Walton makes 21 of 22 shots and scores 44 points to lead UCLA to a record seventh-consecutive title. For the tournament Walton makes 45 of his 59 field goals, an astronomical 76.3%.

Notre Dame 71, UCLA 70

JANUARY 19, 1974 • ATHLETIC AND CONVOCATION CENTER, SOUTH BEND Guard Dwight Clay hits a jump shot from the right corner with :28 left to keep the Irish undefeated and snap UCLA's winning streak—the longest in men's college history—at 88. Clay's basket capped an unlikely comeback from a 70–59 deficit in the game's final 3½ minutes.

North Carolina 96, Duke 92 (OT)

MARCH 2, 1974 • CARMICHAEL AUDITORIUM, CHAPEL HILL, N.C. Trailing by eight points with just 17 seconds left, the Tar Heels mount a historic comeback, scoring twice after forcing turnovers on inbounds plays and then tying the game on a desperate 35-foot heave by freshman Walter Davis that banks in at the buzzer. Davis then scores six of his team's 10 points in extra time to seal the win.

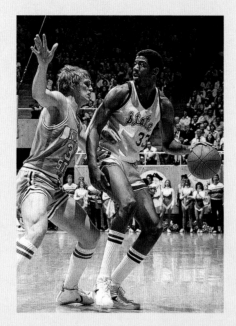

N.C. State 80, UCLA 77 (2OT)

MARCH 23, 1974 • ARENA, GREENSBORO, N.C. Days after he was rushed to the emergency room with a concussion and gash on his neck from a fall in the regional final, David Thompson scores the game's final four points on a jumper and two free throws to hand UCLA it's first tournament loss in 39 tries. Bill Walton scores 29 points, but the Bruins' championship streak ends at seven.

Marquette 67, North Carolina 59

MARCH 28, 1977 • THE OMNI, ATLANTA Trailing Marquette by 12 in the title game, the Tar Heels rally using pressure and fast breaks to take a 45–43 lead with 13:48 left, but then go into their delay game—and it backfires. Marquette's quicker defenders force several turnovers and make 14 free throws to steal the title.

∧ Michigan State 75, Indiana State 64

MARCH 26, 1979 • SPECIAL EVENTS CENTER, SALT LAKE CITY In the most highly anticipated—and most watched—final ever, Spartans sophomore Earvin (Magic) Johnson (*above*) scores a game-high 24 points to Larry Bird's 19 and his supporting cast is better, as Michigan State forward Greg Kelser adds 19 in the win.

GAME CHANGER
BOB KNIGHT
THE MOTION OFFENSE

The ultimate coaching disciplinarian, most notably as a three-time NCAA champion at Indiana from 1971 through 2000, the General devised a scheme that highlights cutting, screening and crisp passing (often, as in the diagram on the right, on the interior), all in reaction to what the defense does. While not an end in itself, movement nevertheless is expected to yield the best shot. The dribble is deemphasized. One dividend: Since there's no planned sequence of movement, the motion offense is all but unscoutable.

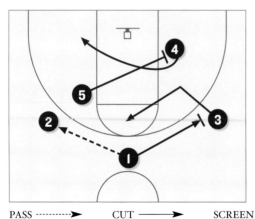

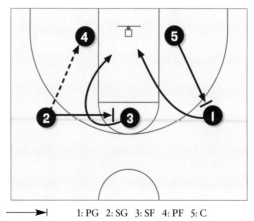

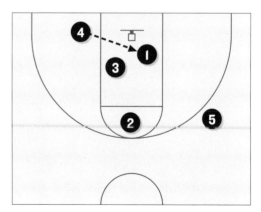

PASS ---------->   CUT ———>   SCREEN ———>| 1: PG   2: SG   3: SF   4: PF   5: C

>> TIME CAPSULE

THE MAN During his three-year varsity career at N.C. State (1972–75), David Thompson averaged 26.8 points and 8.1 rebounds (despite being just 6' 4"), and he so popularized the alley-oop play that he earned the nickname Skywalker. He was an inspiration to many but influenced one North Carolina youngster in particular: Michael Jordan cited Thompson as the player he tried to style his game around, and when he was enshrined in the Hall of Fame he had Thompson introduce him.

THE WOMAN

A 5' 10" point guard from New York City, Nancy Lieberman changed women's basketball. Equal parts flash and fundamentals, she would find the open shooter with a perfect bounce pass or a no-look on the fast break. Leave her open and she'd bury a jumper. A three-time All-America at Old Dominion, Lady Magic led the Monarchs to the 1979 and '80 AIAW national championships.

THE STREAK John Wooden's UCLA Bruins went two years, 11 months and 20 days without a defeat, beginning with a win on Jan. 30, 1971, against UC–Santa Barbara and ending with a 71–70 loss to Notre Dame on Jan. 19, 1974. That loss was particularly disorienting for center Bill Walton. With a 49-game winning streak to end his high school career and an undefeated season on UCLA's freshman team, he went more than five years without losing a single game.

THE CINDERELLA Sun Belt champion Charlotte was in just its seventh Division I season in 1977 when it made its first NCAA tournament appearance, but center Cedric (Cornbread) Maxwell lifted the 49ers to stunning wins over Syracuse by 22 points, then top-ranked Michigan for an improbable trip to the Final Four, where the 49ers lost on a last-second shot to Marquette.

Toing and 'froing at UCLA in 1970.

BASKETBALL BABYLON
CLEMSON'S CHICANERY

The usual ways of breaking rules and ignoring ethics—academic fraud, payments to players, cars for recruits—weren't enough for Clemson, the ACC doormat that jumped into the Top 20 for the first time ever in 1974–75 under coach Tates Locke. One particular Locke stunt lives on in re-cruiting infamy: His phony black fraternity helped lure black players to the lily-white campus, then ceased to exist when their recruiting visits ended. That and a reported $60,000 in payments helped bring in 7' 1" Tree Rollins *(left)*, who led Clemson's turnaround. They also attracted an NCAA inves-tigation and three years probation for the Tigers.

2 Times Centenary College center Robert Parish "unofficially" won the NCAA rebounding title, with 15.4 a game in '74–75 and 18.0 in '75–76. Declared ineligible on an academic technicality, his records are not recognized by the NCAA.

4 Undefeated seasons during the 1970s—two by UCLA (1971–72, '72–73), one for Indiana ('75–76) and N.C. State ('72–73).

115 Combined points for LSU's Pete Maravich (64) and Kentucky's Dan Issel (51) in Wildcats' 121–105 win on Feb. 21, 1970, a single-game record.

$1.5M Contract signed by center Jim Chones who left 21–0 Marquette on Feb. 19, 1972 to join the ABA New York Nets. Marquette lost in the second round of the NCAAs.

100.3 Points per game scored by Jacksonville in 1969–70 to become the first Division I team to average triple digits.

35.1M Number of viewers who tuned in to NBC to watch Larry Bird and Magic Johnson in the 1979 title game. The 24.1 rating and 38 share make it the most watched college game ever.

2009 | COLLISION INSURANCE was in order when Texas Tech's Michael Prince and Oklahoma's Blake Griffin met in Lubbock. | *Photograph by* GREG NELSON

1995 | THE GREEN WAVE hit a Big Blue wall when Tulane's Antonio Jackson tried to score on Kentucky's Walter McCarty (40) in a Wildcats NCAA tournament win. | *Photograph by* JOHN BIEVER

PHIL JACKSON
F, North Dakota 1964–67
NBA Coaching Wins: 1,155

College of Coaches

Before they moved to the sidelines in suits, the seven alltime winningest NBA coaches all got their starts as take–charge players at the collegiate level

 **DON NELSON**
F, Iowa 1959–62
NBA Coaching Wins: 1,335

LENNY WILKENS
G, Providence 1957–60
NBA Coaching Wins: 1,332

JERRY SLOAN
G, Evansville 1962–65
NBA Coaching Wins: 1,221

PAT RILEY
G, Kentucky 1964–67
NBA Coaching Wins: 1,210

LARRY BROWN
G, North Carolina 1960–63
NBA Coaching Wins: 1,098

GEORGE KARL
G, North Carolina 1969–73
NBA Coaching Wins: 1,036

THE SPIRIT OF '76

BY JACK McCALLUM

Thirty-five years after their perfect run to an NCAA title, the Indiana Hoosiers remain the last team to finish an entire season without a single loss. —*from* SI, MARCH 19, 2001

INDIANA'S UNDEFEATED 1975–76 season was in fact the continuation of a championship drive that had begun in '74–75. It's axiomatic around Bloomington that the '74–75 Hoosiers were better than the team that won the title. But a broken left arm suffered by All-America forward Scott May late in the regular season and a fired-up Kentucky team had combined to give Indiana its only defeat, 92–90, in the '75 Mideast Regional final. (Bob Knight's greatest accomplishment was not going 32–0 in 1975–76; it was going 63–1 over two seasons, including two straight unbeaten Big Ten campaigns.) But that loss filled the Hoosiers with motivation. "Because of the disappointment we felt after the Kentucky game," says Quinn Buckner, the point guard on both teams, "we gave ourselves up to the idea of winning it all."

Give they did. Though he shone in the '76 tournament, forward Tom Abernethy did almost nothing but garbage work the entire regular season. Still, he scored more than Buckner and Bobby Wilkerson, both of whom averaged single figures in a defense-minded backcourt. Kent Benson was an All-America center, but in 10 games he had 10 or fewer shot attempts. May, the player of the year that season, was the only Hoosier with what amounted to carte blanche on offense, but Knight made sure he wiped his feet on May's back from time to time. "He'd call me in before practice and tell me he was going to go after me to send a message," says May, "and that's exactly what he did."

With a number of close calls, the Hoosiers made it to the title game in Philadelphia with their perfect record intact, but there they faced the challenge of beating Big Ten rival Michigan for the third time that season. If Indiana was looking for omens, it got a bad one the day before the final. Early in the morning, assistant coach Bob Donewald discovered to his horror that a manager had packed the previous year's Michigan game films but not the ones from the two games in '75–76. He called back to Indiana and got someone from the School of Aviation to fly the film from Bloomington to Philly on a university plane. "We were only about an hour late for the meeting," recalls Donewald. "Bob was so dumbfounded I had acted on my own authority—I don't even want to think about how much it cost—that he didn't say anything to me."

Then, three minutes into the game, Wilkerson got clubbed in the temple by an elbow from Wolverines forward Wayman Britt. Wilkerson was out cold, and the game was held up for about eight minutes before he was taken off on a stretcher. He was transported to a nearby hospital, where he wouldn't allow a nurse to take off his uniform. "Maybe I thought I'd be getting back in," he says.

The next thing Wilkerson remembers was staring up at bedside visitors Knight and John Havlicek, Knight's former Ohio State teammate. To this day Wilkerson has never seen a videotape or heard a replay of the final. "It would hurt too much," he says. Out on the court, meanwhile, the Hoosiers had to regroup. "I'm sure our fans were freaking out and thinking, Oh, no, they're going to fall short again," says Abernethy. "But, honestly, as a team, I don't think we thought that at all." Nonetheless, Michigan had a 35–29 halftime lead.

As May recalls it, this was the entirety of Knight's halftime speech: "If you guys want to be champions and make history, you got 20 minutes to prove it." Then he walked out.

Knight's message got through. Over the final 10 minutes, Buckner (16 points, eight rebounds, four assists for the game) played his best basketball of the season, and May (26 points) and Benson (25 points) were all but unstoppable. As the final seconds ticked away in the victory, both Buckner and May went into impromptu victory dances.

Buckner said he screamed so loud that he almost passed out. The crusade had lasted two years, the release was exquisite. However, in the full bloom of youth none of the players realized how special the moment was. Not until years later, when most of their pro careers had proven to be less satisfying than their four years at Knight U, and not until they had seen team after team fall short of perfection, did it hit them. "To have been part of such a great team with such great guys, and to have had Coach Knight as my mentor, well, that's a tremendous honor and a humbling experience," says Benson.

The Hoosiers of 1975–76 profess not to care if another unbeaten champion emerges, though May adds this: "I'd like it to be a certain kind of team, one that had grown together, learned together, suffered together, had a procession of experiences to get to the top." He smiles. "You don't find that too often today, do you?" . . .

MAY WON player-of-the-year honors and averaged 22.6 points a game in the NCAA tournament as the Hoosiers completed a 63–1 two-year run with a national title.

1980 | NANCY LIEBERMAN (10), with 6' 8" Anne Donovan watching her back, was Lady Magic for AIAW-title-winning Old Dominion. | *Photograph by* COLLEGIATE IMAGES

1973 | LARRY KENON (with arms folded) was dubbed Dr. K at Memphis State, where he surgically took apart foes as he led the Tigers to a championship final. | *Photograph by* RICH CLARKSON

2002 | SAM CLANCY of USC was a surface-to-air missile as he took the ball to the rim with force against Billy Knight of crosstown rival UCLA. | *Photograph by* JOHN W. MCDONOUGH

1996 | ANTOINE WALKER (far right) was poised for a putback over Syracuse's Otis Hill in Kentucky's title-game takeout of the Orange. | *Photograph by* DAVID E. KLUTHO

WELCOME TO HIS WORLD

BY FRANK DEFORD

Al McGuire was at the top of his profession in 1976, yet claimed that he wanted desperately to get out. Four months later, he would lead Marquette to the national championship, and just like that he'd be gone. —*from* SI, NOVEMBER 29, 1976

IN AL MCGUIRE'S OFFICE AT Marquette, images of sad clowns abound. Pictures, all over the place, of sad clowns. Everybody must ask him about them. McGuire is touted to be a con man, so the sad clowns have got to be a setup. Right away, commit yourself to those sad clowns, you're coming down his street. *Hey, buddy, why do you have a banana in your ear? Because I couldn't find a carrot.* Zap, like that. And yet, how strange an affectation: sad clowns. Obviously, they must mean something. It cannot be the sadness, though. Of all the things this fascinating man is—and clown is one—he is not sad.

Another thing he is is street smart. McGuire has grown up and left the pavement for the boardrooms, so now when he spots this quality in others, he calls it "credit-card-wise." One time in a nightclub, when the band played *Unchained Melody*, all the 40-year-olds in the place suddenly got up and packed the floor, cheek to cheek. Nostalgia ran rampant. Right away, Al said, "Summer song. This was a summer song when it came out. Always more memories with summer songs."

Perfect. He got it. Right on the button. Of course this is a small thing. A completely insignificant thing. But the point is, he got it just right. And this is a gift. It is McGuire's seminal gift, for all his success flows from it. The best ballplayers see things on the court. McGuire lacked this ability as an athlete, but he owns it in life. Most people play defense in life, others "token it" (as Al says), but there are few scorers, and even fewer playmakers, guys who see things about to open up and can take advantage. McGuire is one of life's playmakers. He perceives. He should be locked in a bicentennial time capsule so that generations yet unborn will understand what this time was really like. There will be all the computers and radar ovens and Instamatics, and McGuire will pop out from among them in 2176 and say, "If the waitress has dirty ankles, the chili will be good." And, "Every obnoxious fan has a wife at home who dominates him." And, "If a guy takes off his wristwatch before he fights, he means business." And, "Blacks will have arrived only when we start seeing black receptionists who aren't good-looking."

Words tumble from his mouth. Often as not, thoughts are bracketed by the name of the person he is addressing, giving a sense of urgency to even mundane observations: "Tommy, you're going to make the turn here, Tommy." "Howie, how many of these go out, Howie?" And likewise, suddenly, late at night, apropos of nothing, unprompted, spoken in some awe and much gratitude: "Frank, what a great life I've had, Frank."

This starts to get us back to the sad clowns. The key to understanding McGuire is to appreciate his unqualified love of life, of what's going on around him. With him everything is naturally vivid and nearly everything is naturally contradictory, the way it must be in crowded, excited worlds.

So with the clowns. It is not the sadness that matters, or even the clownishness. It is the sad clown, a contradiction. By definition, can there be such a thing as a sad clown? Or a wise coach?

The fans and the press think of McGuire as the berserk hothead who drew two technicals in an NCAA championship game, or the dapper sharpie, playing to the crowd, cursing his players. The fans and the press overlook the fact that McGuire's Marquette teams have made the NCAA or the NIT 10 years in a row, averaging 25 wins a season the last nine, and they got there by concentrating on defense, ice-picking out victories by a few points a game. As a coach, you can't much control an offense: *They just weren't going in for us tonight.* A defense is a constant, seldom fluctuating, always commanding. Just because people see Al McGuire's body on the bench, they assume that is he, carrying on. You want to see Al McGuire, look out on the court, look at the way his team plays, calculating. McGuire will play gin rummy against anybody; he won't play the horses or a wheel in Vegas; he won't play the house. You play him, his game, his world. "People say it's all an act, and maybe it is," he says. "Not all of it—but I don't know myself anymore whether I'm acting. Not anymore. I don't know. I just know it pleases me."

HE WAS born on Sept. 7, 1928 in the Bronx but grew up in the Rockaway Beach section of Queens, where his family ran a workingman's bar. It was a club, a phone, a bank; they cashed paychecks. Al was named for Al Smith, then running as the first major Catholic presidential candidate. Smith was the quintessential New Yorker. He was fervently opposed to Prohibition, wore a derby hat and said such strange words as "raddio," for what brought us *Amos 'n' Andy*. The namesake McGuire, removed from New York for two decades now, first in North Carolina, then in

AN ICONOCLAST unlike any coach to come along before or since, McGuire molded teams in his own image—blue-collar, rebellious and successful.

Milwaukee, still honors the other Al by talking Noo Yawkese. The *r*'s in the middle of many words evaporate. Thus, the fowuds play in the conner, from whence they participate in pattuns.

McGuire also claims to have enriched the language. It was his interest in the stock market, he says, that brought the term "blue chip" into sports ("But I wasn't famous enough at the time to get credit for it"). Likewise, "uptick," for when a stock/team advances. Gambling, a familiar pursuit of his father's, an illness for his legendary older brother John, provided "a push" (a stand-off) and "numbers," the word McGuire invariably uses for dollars.

But it is his imagery, original and borrowed, that is the most vivid McGuire. Seashells and balloons: happiness, victory. Yellow ribbons and medals: success in recruiting. Memos and pipes: academia. Hot bread and gay waiters: guaranteed, a top restaurant. A straw hat in a blizzard: what some people, like the NCAA, will provide you with. Even a whale comes up for a blow sometimes: advice to players who can't get their minds off women. Hot lunch for orphans: a giveaway, some sort of PR venture. French pastry: anything showy or extraneous. Keepers: good-looking broads (you don't throw them back). Closers: people who get by the French pastry and complete a deal, e.g., yours truly, Al McGuire. Guys who charge up the hill into a machine gun: most X-and-O coaches; see also "Brooks Brothers types" and "First Communion guys." Welcome to my world: come uptown with me.

While coaching is his profession, it has never been the ultimate. As a consequence, he is not vulnerable there. McGuire often says (indeed, he doth protest too much), "I've never blown a whistle, looked at a film, worked at a blackboard or organized a practice in my life." Which is true, and which drives other coaches up the wall. He is not friendly with many coaches. Hank Raymonds has been beside him on the bench all 12 years at Marquette and has never had a meal at the McGuires'. Raymonds and young Rick Majerus do the X's and O's, the trench work. McGuire believes in "complementary" coaches, as he does in complementary players, units that support each other's efforts, not duplicate them. "I can drink enough cocktails for the whole staff," McGuire says. "I don't need another me."

"People can't understand my players screaming back at me," he says, "but it's healthy. Also, I notice that the scream-

ing always comes when we're 15, 20 ahead. When it's tied, then they're all listening very carefully to what I have to say."

Many adult coaches demand unquestioning loyalty from 20-year-old kids. As McGuire points out, some of the most successful coaches even refuse to accept kids with different philosophies, conflicting egos. "Dealing with problems, with differences—that is what coaching is," he says. "Running pattuns is not coaching." He does not believe that character can be "built" with haircuts and Marine routines and by coaches so insecure that their players can never challenge them.

Off the court, McGuire sees his players only when they come to him in distress. He would be suspicious of any college kid who wanted to be buddy-buddy with a middle-aged man, and vice versa. "I don't pamper," he says. "These guys are celebrities in their own sphere of influence—top shelf, top liquor. Everybody around them touches them with clammy hands. That's the only word: clammy. Well, they don't get that from me." Often, he doesn't even bother to learn their names. For much of last season the starting center, Jerome Whitehead, was called Chapman. Sometimes McGuire has stood up to scream at a player and then had to sink back down because he couldn't remember the kid's name.

Everyone assumes McGuire gets along with his players—especially the inner-city blacks—because of his unique personality. But look past the French pastry and his calculation surfaces again, just as he promises. No con works unless the conned party figures he is the one really getting the edge. McGuire settles for a push. "They get and I get," he says. While the players don't get an uncle-coach, they get, as McGuire calls it, "a post-recruiter." He virtually forces them to get a diploma, and he hustles them up the richest pro contracts or good jobs in business. It is surely not just a coincidence that McGuire has thrived during the years when the big-money pro war was on. He has been a cash coach in a cash-and-carry era.

Shamelessly, McGuire promotes his seniors, a ploy that keeps a kid hustling, playing defense, giving up the ball for his first three seasons, so he will get the ball and the shots (and maybe then the big numbers) his final year.

"I figure I'm wrong 80 percent of the time," McGuire says, "but it takes too much time to be right. I won't pay that price with my life. I'm jealous of guys like Dean Smith, Bobby

THE SAD clowns on the walls of McGuire's office at Marquette were a perfect symbol of the coach's contradictory nature.

Knight. I'm jealous of their dedication. I wish I had it. I admire the way their teams are dressed, the way their kids handle themselves. At the regionals last year one of our kids came down to lunch barefoot. But I just don't like coaching that much to put the time in on a thing like that. It's not my world. I run my team the only way I can run it and still keep my life."

The McGuire Arrangement is, basically, us-against-them—"The only two things blacks have ever dominated are basketball and poverty"—and it works because he tends bar for everybody. Nobody ever fussed with McGuire more than last year's ball handler, Lloyd Walton. "Sit down!" he would scream at his coach all through games. Says Walton, "He figures your problems are his problems. Hey, I've had a black coach in summer ball, but I never had the rapport with him I had with Al."

When McGuire learned one November night back in 1968 that revolutionaries on campus were pressuring the black players to quit because they were being "exploited," he met with the players in a motel room sometime after 2 a.m. He didn't go long on philosophy. He told them he would support their decision if they left and gave up their scholarships, but he also reminded them that there were more where they came from—maybe not so good, but they weren't Marquette basketball. He was.

Then he faced down the radicals. The smooth-talking theorists he screamed at. The tough guys he ridiculed. He suggested to an idealistic white coed that she should take one of the black players home to her suburb for Thanksgiving. To a priest, he snarled, "Don't come after these kids from the Jesuit house. You never bought a pound of butter in your life, and you're asking them to be kamikaze pilots." By 4:30 a.m., the revolution was dead.

The relationship between Marquette and McGuire is a curious one and, it seems, a push. Marquette is one of the few Catholic schools left—Notre Dame, St. John's and the U. of San Francisco are others—that compete, year after year, with the huge state institutions. For that matter, Marquette is the only private school of any stripe that is always right there at the top. The Warriors not only sell out for the season, they do it head to head, in the same building, against the Milwaukee Bucks, which until recently have been a first-class pro team.

Of course, there are certain Marquette elements leery of the image of the school being filtered through the McGuire prism.

What the nation sees of Marquette University is a self-proclaimed hustler, ranting and raving at the Establishment, running a team of ghetto blacks dressed in wild uniforms. What is this, some kind of desperado vocational school? In fact Marquette is a relatively subdued place, Jesuit, stocked for the most part by white middle-class Midwestern Catholics who end up as schoolteachers. Typically, McGuire—who sent all three of his children there—guarantees that it must be good academically or it couldn't get by charging such high tuition numbers.

While the coach and the school do share the same religion, McGuire does not get faith confused with the pattuns or the players who execute them. His only public concession to Catholicism, such as it is, is his pregame exhortation, which went like this last season, all in one breath: "All-right-let's-show-them-we're-the-Number-2-team-in-the-country-and-beat-the-bleep-out-of-them-Queen-of-Victory-pray-for-us."

How could a guy so Noo Yawk fit in so well in Milwaukee, or in Carolina before that? It's easy. Wherever McGuire is, he constructs a whole universe out of selected bars and restaurants, places to walk, teddy bears and zanies, back rooms and penthouses, motorcycles and country-music jukeboxes. Tall guys with broken noses are also a part of this community. There is a cast and there are sets—everything but a zip code.

Nobody else is permitted to see it all. He tells his secretaries when he hires them: two years. After two years, no matter how good you are—especially if you're good—out. The only person who lives in Al McGuireland is Al McGuire. Cynics and the jealous take a look at the characters who pass through and they check out his con and whisper that he is really an ice-cold man who surrounds himself with bootlickers and sycophants. But that is not true. On the contrary. Sure, they all play up to McGuire—remember now, charmers are an overlay—but he has a need for them too. Not just the players and the coaches, but all the people and places in Al McGuireland are complementary. Like his players, all retain their individuality and integrity. That's the whole point: otherwise they're no good to him. Lloyd Walton screaming back is the Lloyd Walton that McGuire wants.

Critics say it is all an act. McGuire wonders himself. But, no, he is not acting. He is directing all the time. Al, you're a director, Al. You're always running pattuns. . . .

MCGUIRE ROLLED with the fashions of the time, but he depended heavily on the solid, conservative coaches to his right, Hank Raymonds and Rick Majerus.

1945 | AN EXTRA rim, called a Keaney ring after its originator, challenged St. John's Ivor Sumner to become a more accurate shooter. | *Photograph by* GJON MILI

1973 | FLY WILLIAMS (with ball) practiced on the netless rims of Brooklyn playgrounds, but he became one of the nation's top scorers at Austin Peay. | *Photograph by* JOHN D. HANLON

2009 | THE REFEREE got an imploring thumbs-up from Kansas's Mario Little, who was looking for a jump ball in a win over Oklahoma State. | *Photograph by* JAMIE SQUIRE

2002 | T.J. FORD of Texas did the downward-facing Longhorn as he was sent head over heels by Georgia's Damien Wilkins in a Texas win. | *Photograph by* CHRIS HAMPSON

FLYING TO THE TOP

BY BRUCE NEWMAN

Even late in his senior year, Indiana State's Larry Bird was a mystery to most college basketball fans, owing to a lack of TV coverage and his own retiring nature. —*from* SI, FEBRUARY 5, 1979

THE PHONE HAD BEEN SITTING there, stubbornly refusing to ring for what must have been a minute or more, when Ed McKee, the sports information director at Indiana State, finally began to stare disbelievingly at it. CBS Radio had just called, and before that *The Providence Journal*, and in between there were a lot of questions by an insistent chap from the *New York Post*. "They all want to talk to Larry Bird," McKee said glumly, as the phone finally rang. "And Larry's not talking."

This time the call was from Nancy Petersen of the National Solid Waste Association. You know, garbage. Petersen said that the Solid Waste people wanted to do a feature on Bird for their monthly newsletter because they had heard that he used to work on a garbage truck back in his hometown of French Lick, Ind. That was four years ago, when Bird was trying to make up his mind whether to go back to college so he could become a zillionaire in the NBA or pursue a career as a filling-station attendant. Petersen told McKee that she would need an interview with Bird and would also like a picture of Larry "doing a dunk." McKee promised to see what he could do and hung up.

Well, hey, Nancy Petersen, tell the National Solid Waste Association, and the man from Glad, and anybody else who happens to ask, there ain't no flies on the Indiana State Sycamores. Last week they ran their record to 18–0 with a 77–69 win over Creighton that not only allowed them to remain undefeated, but also came on the same day as losses by top-rated Notre Dame and No. 2 North Carolina. As Indiana State stood trembling on the threshold of the No. 1 spot in college basketball, a lot of people who don't live in Terre Haute—which is where the Indiana State campus is located—were suddenly wondering: Who are those guys?

There are several good reasons why Indiana State has been the best-kept secret in basketball this year, and all of them trace back to Bird. Going into last week, he was the nation's leading scorer, with 31.0 points a game, and stood third in rebounding, with 15.0 a game.

Bird, a 6' 9½" forward, was considered such an extraordinary pro prospect that the Celtics used a first-round pick in last June's NBA draft to select him, hoping they either could persuade him to skip his senior year or sign him this spring before the 1979 draft is held on June 25. Last summer, his talks with the Celtics dragged on so long that NBC's schedule of national games-of-the-week was announced before anyone knew if he would return to school. The result is that, unless NBC suddenly revises its schedule, Indiana State will appear on nationwide television only if it makes the NCAA tournament semifinals next month. "Should we ever get on national TV," says Sycamores coach Bill Hodges. "I imagine the first thing that would surprise a lot of people is that Larry Bird is a white guy."

They would also find he's not especially loquacious. When he agreed to return for his final year of college, his one requirement was that he not be forced to talk to the press. Bird has never trusted strangers who ask a lot of nosy questions. His life has been fraught with a series of personal tragedies and feelings of inadequacy. When he was a high school senior, he was recruited by a Florida college and was sent a plane ticket so he could visit the school. But when Bird arrived at the airport, he took one look at the airplane on the runway and was so frightened at the idea of flying that he turned right around and went home.

Bird then decided to attend Indiana University, which has an enrollment of 31,500; it took him only a week to realize that he was in over his head, and once again he bolted for home. Shortly after leaving Indiana, he enrolled at Northwood Institute, a 160-student junior college in West Baden, Ind., but he quit again, after only two months. "He was very unsettled," says Northwood coach Jack Johnson. "He had trouble attending class and was very undisciplined."

For the remainder of what would have been his freshman year, Bird had a job with the French Lick parks department, which included a stint on the celebrated garbage truck. It was during that year that Bird's father committed suicide, after which Larry was persuaded to return to school by Indiana State's recruiters. A brief marriage followed, but that ended in divorce in September of 1976. There were attempts at a reconciliation, but the only thing that resulted was a paternity suit—filed against Bird by his former wife, Janet.

"Basketball is my whole life and it will always be my whole life," Bird has said. "I'm a lot smarter on the court than I am in life." . . .

BIRD TOOK Indiana State to its first Division I NCAA tournament and carried it all the way to the national championship game in his senior year.

Unsung, Unloved . . . and Essential

If they're noticed at all, it's usually to be heaped with abuse, but the referees bring order to the chaos of the college game—sometimes with flair, sometimes not, but always with integrity

2008 | MIKE WOOD

2006 | KARL HESS

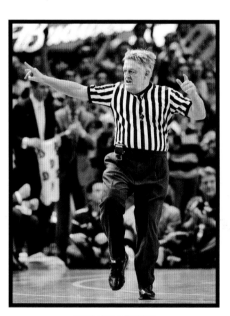

2010 | JIM BURR

2009 | TONY GREENE

2007 | PAUL JANSSEN

2010 | MIKE SANZERE

1998 | IT WAS hog taunting zebra as Arkansas's mascot, Big Red, tested the eyesight—and the sense of humor—of an SEC ref who went along with the joke. | *Photograph by* PHIL HUBER

2011 | THE NEARNESS of youth is one of the pitfalls of dealing with the Cameron Crazies at Duke, as Carolina freshman Harrison Barnes learned the hard way. | *Photograph by* BOB ROSATO

A TALENT OF BIBLICAL PROPORTIONS

BY GRANT WAHL

Midway through his first and only season, Texas's Kevin Durant had already staked his claim to the Wooden and Naismith player of the year awards, neither of which had ever before been won by a freshman. —*from* SI, FEBRUARY 19, 2007

H E'S JUST A BABY, ALL ARMS and legs as thin as capellini. Kevin Durant only turned 18 in September, but with his soft, open face he could pass for 15. After a recent loss the Texas freshman walked to meet the press clutching the right hand of his mother, Wanda Pratt, who says she can tell when her son is distraught because "he'll call me Mommy instead of Mom" in text messages. On most nights, just before bedtime, Durant will kneel down to pray and digest a few more pages from a personalized Bible. Asked which book he's reading, Durant flashes a look of palpable pride.

"Numbers," he says.

Funny, those aren't the numbers that most of us mortals associate with Durant, the 6' 9" forward whose coltish coming-of-age has put the man in freshman during a historic college season. Take your pick of diabolical digits. Maybe it's K-Smoove's 25.1 points and 11.4 rebounds a game, which make him the only player in the nation's Top 5 in both categories. Maybe it's the mid-eight-figure shoe deal and the multimillion dollar NBA contract that await whenever he decides to turn pro, probably this spring. Maybe it's his pterodactyl-like 7' 6" wingspan. Or maybe it's just a simple zero, which happens to be the number of freshmen in the annals of college hoops who've been named national player of the year.

Until, perhaps, 2006–07. "I've had so many people tell me he's the best player in college basketball," Longhorns coach Rick Barnes says of Durant, who'd had an astonishing six 30-plus-point barrages in 10 Big 12 games through Sunday. "People have a hard time saying that because he's a freshman, but class has nothing to do with it. If I went into this season knowing we didn't have a point guard and had said, 'Kevin, you have to be our point guard,' he could have done that. If I said to him,

'You've got to be a low-post player and stay there,' Kevin would do that. So what we've done this year is let him do all of it."

And even that isn't enough for Durant. Only minutes after he had torched Baylor for 34 points and nine boards in an 84–79 win on Jan. 27, he was almost apologizing for yet another sick box-score line. "I could have played much better, man," he said, shaking his head. "Could have rebounded more, could have played better defense. I just have to improve on my weaknesses."

For years the game's guardians have lamented the sacrifice of American fundamentals at the altar of summer basketball and its glorified pickup games, but Durant's mastery of the basics—his feather-soft shot, his unselfish passing, even his low defensive stance—is a stinging rebuke to those who say it can't be done anymore. None of it happened by accident. "Between the ages of 10 and 16, Kevin put in eight-hour days during the summer [working on basketball drills]," says Taras (Stink) Brown, the coach at the Seat Pleasant (Md.) Activity Center outside Washington. Brown forbade Durant from playing five-on-five during their training sessions so he could concentrate on fundamentals. "Some days I wouldn't pick up a basketball," Durant says. "He'd put 60 minutes on the clock and say I had to do defensive drills the whole time." To toughen up Durant even more, his mother and Brown would make him run sprints up Hunt's Hill, a quad-burner near the rec center that Durant estimates he scaled a thousand times over a six-year period.

Durant's work ethic has only intensified now that he's in Austin. Not only does he start pregame shootarounds 40 minutes before his teammates, lofting jumpers from all over the court, but he'll also show up for Sunday sessions the day after Big 12 road games when Barnes would prefer that he take it easy. If the gold standard for modern freshmen is Carmelo Anthony, who led Syracuse to the 2003 national title, then Durant is hoping he can go platinum by continuing to surpass Melo's regular-season numbers (Anthony averaged 22.2 points and 10.0 rebounds) and matching his '03 postseason feats. "[Syracuse] won the title during my freshman year [of high school]," Durant says. "I watched with my mom, and she said, 'Maybe you could do that one day.' "...

DURANT BROUGHT a rare mix of abilities to Texas, where he was a Top 5 scorer and rebounder and an uncanny marksman, making 40.4% of his three-pointers.

JOE MCNALLY

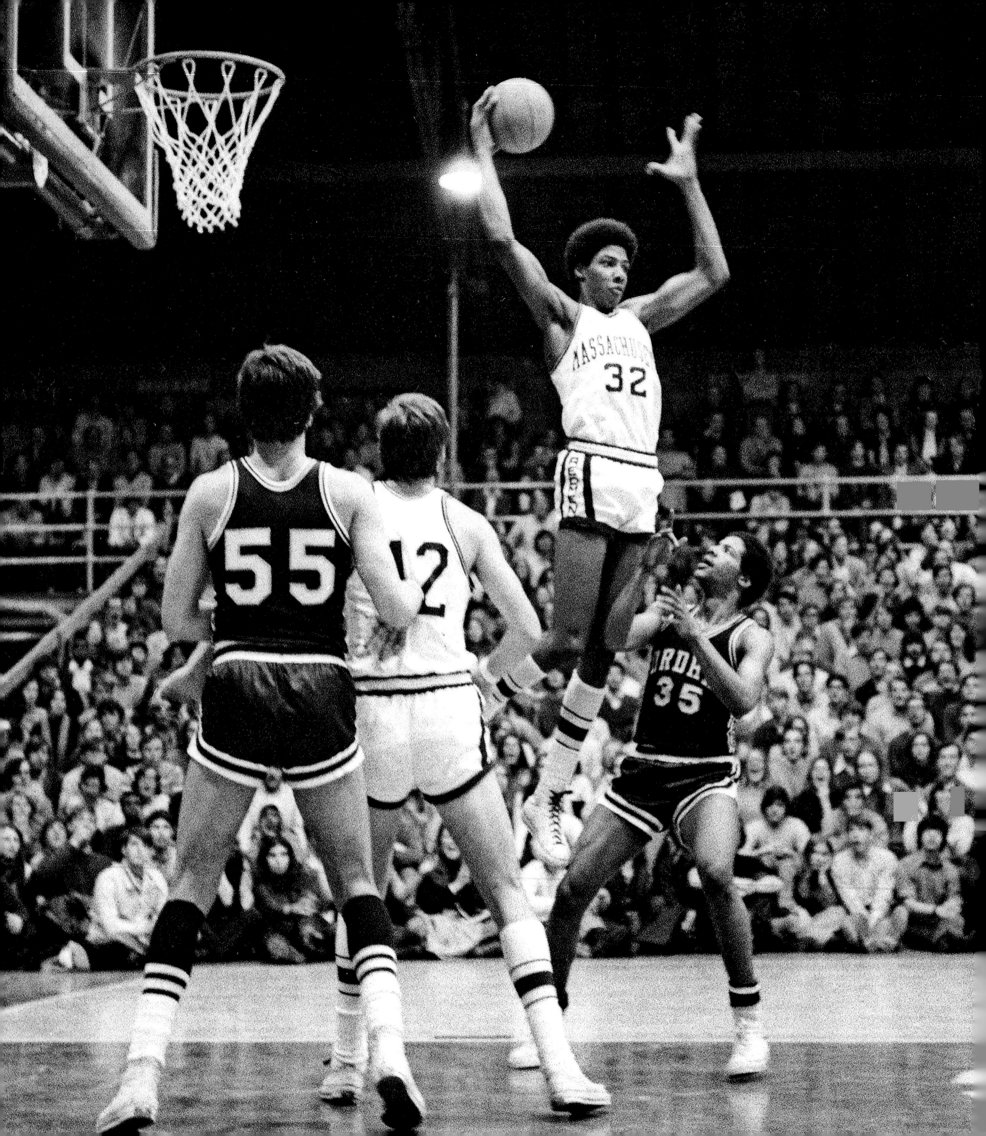

1977 | KYLE MACY (4) was a three-time All-America at Kentucky and a driving force for the Wildcats when they won their first title in 20 years in '78. | *Photograph by* RICH CLARKSON

1971 | JULIUS ERVING became known as Dr. J at UMass, and he operated at a rarified level there, averaging 26.3 points and 20.2 rebounds for two seasons. | *Photograph by* WIL BLANCHE

1978 | THESE FORMAL STARS, all sophomores, were in a historic class of their own: (from left) Ohio State's Herb Williams, Maryland's Albert King, Notre Dame's Kelly Tripucka, Duke's Gene Banks, BYU's Danny Ainge, Kansas's Darnell Valentine, Iona's Jeff Ruland, Virginia's Jeff Lamp, USC's Cliff Robinson and Michigan State's Magic Johnson. | *Photograph by* LANE STEWART

THE
1980s

1982 | IN TIME Charles Barkley would become a rounder Mound of Rebound, but he dominated the boards in the SEC in all three of his seasons at Auburn.

Photograph by MANNY RUBIO

LOCK IS TICKING

1980S, THE MARKETING GENIUSES
a-based soft-drink company decided to secretly tinker with
rmula to their universally beloved beverage. At around the same
time, the people in charge of college hoops noticed that their product could also use tweaking. Scoring had been decreasing drastically. The 1982 ACC title game between North Carolina and Virginia featured such future pro stars as Michael Jordan, Sam Perkins, James Worthy and Ralph Sampson, yet the Tar Heels intermittently stalled and balled to just a 47–45 win.

So along came New Coke in April of 1985. And along came the 45-second shot clock in October of the same year.

One didn't work; Classic Coke was back in stores a few months later. The other did; scoring went up, and those unsightly hold-the-ball games disappeared. The three-point shot was added the following year, and one coach in particular took the new rules and ran with them. Loyola Marymount under Paul Westhead *averaged* 122.4 points a game in 1989–90. For hoops fans, at least, change was refreshing.

Everywhere else, though, cataclysms abounded: the AIDS epidemic; the Union Carbide gas leak in Bhopal (1984); the *Challenger* and Chernobyl disasters (both 1986); Pan Am Flight 103 (1988) and the *Exxon Valdez* oil spill (1989). But just as the decade was about to end, in November of 1989, the biggest change of all came amid great rejoicing. The Wall came down in Berlin.   —J.M.

The Wall's fall would change the world forever.

> All-Decade Teams

MEN'S FIRST TEAM

Michael Jordan
G - NORTH CAROLINA

Steve Alford
G - INDIANA

Danny Manning
F - KANSAS

Sam Perkins
F - NORTH CAROLINA

Ralph Sampson
C - VIRGINIA

WOMEN'S FIRST TEAM

Lynette Woodard
G - KANSAS

Teresa Weatherspoon
G - LOUISIANA TECH

Cheryl Miller
F - USC

Bridgette Gordon
F - TENNESSEE

Anne Donovan
C - OLD DOMINION

NATIONAL CHAMPION		COACH
'80*	LOUISVILLE	Denny Crum
'81	INDIANA	Bob Knight
'82	NORTH CAROLINA	Dean Smith
'83	NORTH CAROLINA STATE	Jim Valvano
'84	GEORGETOWN	John Thompson
'85	VILLANOVA	Rollie Massimino
'86	LOUISVILLE	Denny Crum
'87	INDIANA	Bob Knight
'88	KANSAS	Larry Brown
'89	MICHIGAN	Steve Fisher

*DENOTES YEAR IN WHICH SEASON ENDED

LEADING SCORER		POINTS PER GAME
TONY MURPHY,	Southern	32.1
ZAM FREDRICK,	South Carolina	28.9
HARRY KELLY,	Texas Southern	29.7
HARRY KELLY,	Texas Southern	28.8
JOE JAKUBICK,	Akron	30.1
XAVIER McDANIEL,	Wichita State	27.2
TERRANCE BAILEY,	Wagner	29.4
KEVIN HOUSTON,	Army	32.9
HERSEY HAWKINS,	Bradley	36.3
HANK GATHERS,	Loyola Marymount	32.7

LEADING REBOUNDER		REBOUNDS PER GAME
LARRY SMITH,	Alcorn State	15.1
DARRYL WATSON,	Mississippi Valley State	14.0
LaSALLE THOMPSON,	Texas	13.5
XAVIER McDANIEL,	Wichita State	14.4
AKEEM OLAJUWON,	Houston	13.5
XAVIER McDANIEL,	Wichita State	14.8
DAVID ROBINSON,	Navy	13.0
JEROME LANE,	Pittsburgh	13.5
KENNY MILLER,	Loyola (Ill.)	13.6
HANK GATHERS,	Loyola Marymount	13.7

>> WISH YOU WERE THERE

North Carolina 63, Georgetown 62

MARCH 29, 1982 · LOUISIANA SUPERDOME, NEW ORLEANS
Despite the presence of All-America upperclassmen James Worthy and Sam Perkins, it's freshman Michael Jordan who makes the go-ahead basket when the national championship is on the line, firing in a 16-foot jumper from the left side with 17 seconds left. Georgetown guard Fred Brown then mistakes Worthy for a teammate and passes him the ball with just seven seconds to go, sealing the Heels' victory.

Louisville 80, Kentucky 68 (OT)

MARCH 26, 1983 · STOKELY ATHLETICS CENTER, KNOXVILLE, TENN.
After years of Kentucky refusing to meet Louisville, a mischievous tournament committee puts them on a collision course in the NCAAs' Elite Eight. In the Dream Game, as it's known, Kentucky guard Jim Master sends the game into OT with a buzzer-beating 12-foot jumper, only to have the Cardinals open the overtime with a 14–0 blitz that clinches Commonwealth bragging rights.

North Carolina State 54, Houston 52 ∧

APRIL 4, 1983 · UNIVERSITY ARENA, ALBUQUERQUE In the first 39:59 of the NCAA final, N.C. State forward Lorenzo Charles *(above)* misses

five of six shots against Akeem Olajuwon, but with three seconds left, guard Dereck Whittenburg fires a desperation 35-foot airball and Charles grabs the miss and dunks as time expires to forever rock the basketball world.

Villanova 66, Georgetown 64

APRIL 1, 1985 · RUPP ARENA, LEXINGTON, KY. Ranked no higher than 14th during a 19–10 regular season, eighth-seeded Villanova squeaks through its first three tournament games on the way to meeting defending national champ Georgetown in the final. Needing to play a perfect game, the Wildcats hit 22 of their 28 shots (78.6%) while center Ed Pinckney (16 points, six rebounds) outplays Player of the Year Patrick Ewing (14 points, five boards) in the massive upset.

Indiana 74, Syracuse 73

MARCH 30, 1987 · LOUISIANA SUPERDOME, NEW ORLEANS
After Syracuse forward Derrick Coleman misses the free throw on the front end of a one-and-one that could have sealed a win for the Orangemen, Indiana's Keith Smart buries a corner jumper over the desperate reach of Howard Triche for the game-winner with four seconds left as the Hoosiers nail down their second title of the decade.

GAME CHANGER
DEAN SMITH
THE FOUR CORNERS

In the pre-shot-clock era, the North Carolina guru's tactic when his team had a lead was the ultimate time waster—and a source of high-percentage shots. As the name suggests, four players on offense each take a corner of the court, while the point guard *(1, red)* directs the action. If the defense hangs back, the player with the ball can simply take precious time off the clock. If the foe tries to force the issue, the ballhandler can play keepaway *(left and right diagrams)* or penetrate and pitch to an open man *(middle)*.

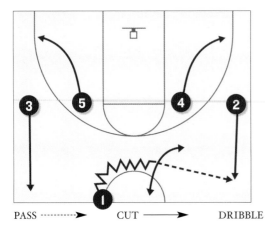
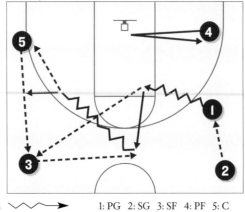
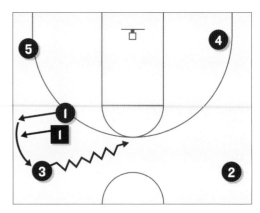

PASS ----------> CUT ——→ DRIBBLE ∿∿∿→ 1: PG 2: SG 3: SF 4: PF 5: C

He remains the career leader in points and rebounds for the storied program.

THE WOMAN Considered by many the greatest female player, Cheryl Miller, a 6' 2" forward from USC, was a four-time All-America and three-time Naismith Player of the Year ('84, '85, '86), while leading the Women of Troy to titles in '83 and '84—winning MVP honors in both Final Fours.

THE CINDERELLA N.C. State in '83 and Villanova in '85 are better known, but LSU in '87 gets the nod for a longer sustained run

Elite Eight. They led Indiana 75–66 with 4:38 to go, but the Hoosiers rallied and won 77–76 on a fluke play when Ricky Calloway grabbed an airball and scored with :07 left.

THE STREAK
LaSalle forward Lionel Simmons, the consensus Player of the Year as a senior in 1989–90, put together the longest string of double-digit scoring games in NCAA history, with 115. The old mark of 112 was held by BYU's Danny Ainge.

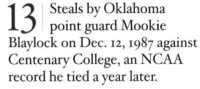

Big hair was in the air at Arizona in 1987.

13 Steals by Oklahoma point guard Mookie Blaylock on Dec. 12, 1987 against Centenary College, an NCAA record he tied a year later.

74.6 Record percentage shot from the field by Oregon State center Steve Johnson in '80–81.

50.8 Percentage shot from beyond the arc by Indiana in '86–87, the only Division I team to make better than half its three-point tries.

3 Times that Southern guard Avery Johnson dished 20 or more assists in games in '87–88 on way to a record 13.3-assist average.

BASKETBALL BABYLON
TROUBLE AT TULANE

In March 1985 star center John (Hot Rod) Williams (*left*) was indicted along with two Tulane teammates on numerous counts of sports bribery and conspiracy for allegedly receiving thousands of dollars in cash in exchange for shaving points. Williams eventually would be acquitted at trial, but during the investigation it was learned that an assistant coach recruited Williams by giving him a shoebox stuffed with $10,000 in cash, and that coach Ned Fowler frequently gave Williams $100 handshakes after he got to Tulane. Embarrassed school president Eamon Kelly disbanded the program for three years before it was revived in 1989.

48 Millions paid by CBS in 1982 for NCAA tournament broadcast rights through 1984, a 70% increase over NBC's previous deal.

1986 | A HEAVENLY touch made a shooting star out of
UCLA's Reggie Miller, who ended his career as the Bruins'
No. 2 alltime scorer | *Photograph by* JOE MCNALLY

2006 | JOAKIM NOAH chased a loose ball and a title with the same single-minded focus as Florida beat UCLA for the first of two straight NCAA crowns. | *Photograph by* JOHN BIEVER

1994 | A LAST-MINUTE three by Arkansas's Scotty Thurman over Antonio Lang was the dagger that did in Duke in the title game. | *Photograph by* JOHN BIEVER

HEY, YOU'D BE HOG WILD, TOO

BY CURRY KIRKPATRICK

No four days in tournament history have done more to inspire the term March Madness than the upset-crazed first two rounds of the '81 NCAAs. —*from* SI, MARCH 23, 1981

AND ANOTHER NCAA tournament goes ka-pow. How?

Comebacks. Kansas State, 12 points behind San Francisco, 11 points behind Oregon State, survived.

Way backs. Arkansas, hogs' hopes deep in the muck of almost certain doom until a guy named U.S. threw one in from halfway across the U.S., survived.

Get backs. LSU and Notre Dame, both still wincing from the stench of last year's tournament embarrassments as well as this year's pre-tourney foldups, survived.

And stand backs. Most of all, stand backs: those magical occasions when fans of college basketball have only to stand back and let its handiwork inimitably unfold. The perfection of Indiana. The versatility of Brigham Young's Danny Ainge. The surprise of Alabama-Birmingham. The shock of Oregon State. The shame—no, not again!—of DePaul.

No matter what happens from now on—and nothing could be more discombobulating than the day 1981's top two seeds and 1980's two finalists went down—there will be no more memorable vision than that of a young coach named Jimmy Lynam, out of southwest Philadelphia by way of *Our Gang*, bounding along the sidelines and finally falling into the arms of Denise Lynam, 15, who was weeping and laughing concurrently because of St. Joseph's 49–48 victory over No. 1 DePaul only seconds before.

Never mind that the Hawks were representing a school with but 2,340 students, which hadn't won a postseason game for 15 years, which had barely beaten American to get into the NCAAs. Never mind that the Hawks may exit the tournament as suddenly as they stunned it. Last Saturday in the Mideast second round at Dayton, the resolute Philadelphians outshot, outhustled, outpoised and outbrained the conceited, haughty Blue Demons. In the end St. Joseph's had dispensed a dose of aspirin to the spoiled children of DePaul which they will remember the rest of their lives.

Even after Lynam had controlled the pace with an offense that sought only short shots, even after the Hawks gone had frustrated the Roberto Duran of campus hoops, DePaul's Mark Aguirre (six shots, eight points, one rebound); even then the heavily favored Demons looked safe leading 42–35 with 11:15 left. But Clyde Bradshaw, the Demons' backcourt catalyst, picked up his fourth foul and coach Ray Meyer's team became cautious, tentative, tight. "We're not going there to have fun," assistant coach Joey Meyer had warned his father before the game. "They were scared."

DePaul, a bad half-court delay team, went into a half-court delay offense. Three stupid, sloppy plays cost DePaul the game. First 6' 8" Teddy Grubbs lost a jump ball to St. Joe's 6' 5" John Smith (remember the name), following which Bryan Warrick hit a jumper to narrow DePaul's lead to a point with 48 seconds left.

After two timeouts during which the DePaul bench became "mass confusion," as the younger Meyer put it, the Demons barely got the ball in bounds to Skip Dillard, who acted as if it were the last thing he wanted. He was fouled anyway at :13. While Dillard, nicknamed Money for his .851 foul shooting, thought a while— "I've dreamed all my life about being in that situation," he said later—young whippersnapper Lynam set the Hawks up for what he called a "scramble situation": Get the rebound, race downcourt, no timeout, spread yourselves, take a good shot. Which is exactly what happened after Money Dillard, dreaming, did indeed miss.

On the scorecards it was St. Joseph's Warrick racing on the dribble (as Aguirre gave up on him at midcourt in a "*no más*" defense) to freshman Lonnie McFarlan open at the right corner baseline, to John Smith (you remembered) all alone underneath for the winning layup. "Just an ordinary Fourth and Shunk [a Philly playground] number," said Smith, who had summoned McFarlan's pass by yelling, simply, "Please."

As Aguirre walked off toward downtown Dayton and probably the NBA with his stereo earphones shutting out the world, Ray Meyer could be forgiven if he was thinking, Thanks again, Mark, but please go ahead and turn pro and leave this marvelously talented team to fend for itself, find its soul elsewhere and maybe discover some character in the clutch. "I'm supposed to have the team of my life," Meyer had said. "But I can't enjoy 'em. I never know whether these kids are going to loaf or put out. Honest to God, I never thought basketball was going to be this way again."

Que será, Ray. And so long, again. . . .

TWO DePAUL defenders looked on helplessly as St. Joe's Lonnie McFarlan passed inside for a game-winning layup, sending the top-seeded Blue Demons home early.

1991 | SHAQUILLE O'NEAL didn't mind playing the class clown in his two All-America seasons at LSU, but he later returned to school to get his degree. | *Photograph by* JODI BUREN

1990 | STACEY AUGMON (left) and Larry Johnson put UNLV on the road to a new level of respectability with their championship-winning season as juniors. | *Photograph by* JEAN MOSS

2010 | KANSAS'S INBOUNDS passer put his best foot forward against UCLA as he got the ball to Tyrel Reed in a matchup of college colossi at Allen Fieldhouse. | *Photograph by* BILL FRAKES

YOU ALL RIGHT?" IT WAS AN odd thing for a coach to say to a player who was about to shoot two hugely important free throws. It was an odder thing still for a coach to say to a player who on seven previous occasions that evening had launched the ball from the foul line into the ether of the Hoosier Dome and smartly through the hoop. Given the circumstances—12 seconds to play against mighty UNLV, tie game, a shot at the national title game in the balance—it may have been oddest of all that the player, Christian Laettner of Duke, grinned back.

Let the coach, Mike Krzyzewski, explain: "Two years earlier we had met as a team after losing to Seton Hall at the '89 Final Four in Seattle. I was determined not to lay any guilt trips on the players, not to let them leave that room feeling down. I told them we were staying through the championship game to celebrate what they had accomplished. Then I looked at my seniors and I started to cry.

"Laettner is sitting right in front of me. He's only 19. He's bewildered. I'm not sure he's ever seen an adult cry. And later that night—it must have been 11 o'clock—I'm watching tape in my hotel room and there's this knock at the door. It's Christian. He wants to know if I'm all right. He sits down, and I tell him how proud I am of what they've done and how we would build on it. And again he says, 'Are you sure you're all right?' When he gets up to leave, before he shuts the door, he turns and says, 'You sure you're all right?'

"I threw a pillow at him and said, 'Get out of here.'"

Let other coaches throw chairs. Krzyzewski, the man from rigid and proper Duke, schooled at West Point, purportedly cloned from Bob Knight, will throw pillows. When the NCAA tournament gets under way next week, Krzyzewski will be trying to guide the defending national champion Blue Devils, 25–2 and ranked No. 1 all season, to their sixth trip to the Final Four in seven years.

Krzyzewski has one thing going for him that few other coaches have and that none can acquire by studying tape or spending time

do better by their two boys. ("In my mom's closet there were always two dresses," Krzyzewski says. "They were clean, they were in great shape, but there were only two. My parents were people who never had anything, but they had everything.") Yet he is a card-carrying baby boomer who attended Army as a member of its most restless class, the class of 1969, one that kept a nervous eye on Southeast Asia. Thus even as Krzyzewski relates like some touchie-feely big brother, he's a schoolmaster preaching hoary precepts out of a simpler time, someone who can hammer home a standard coaching exhortation like "Give me the best that you've got" by playing Anita Baker in the locker room.

This peculiar generational straddling act goes a long way toward explaining how Krzyzewski has risen to the summit of his profession. Four times in five years he had gone to the Final Four and fallen short; but he had understood long ago what can be learned from falling short, and he had internalized those lessons even as pundits breezily concluded that it was his fate to be there at the end and preside in gentlemanly fashion over a loss, like some latter-day Bud Grant or Gene Mauch. Couldn't win it all—just as he supposedly couldn't coach in the Atlantic Coast Conference and couldn't recruit in it, couldn't make that Knight shtick work, and had a name that couldn't even be pronounced, for goodness' sake.

He broke through at the '91 Final Four in much the same way he had overcome back-to-back 17-loss seasons at Duke in 1982 and '83 (one of those 34 defeats, a 17-pointer at Princeton in December '81, left him crying in the shower) and much as he had risen above a washout recruiting year in 1981, an epic oh-fer that remains unmatched in the annals of player procurement. In each case he retooled and tried again, and if he flubbed again, he tried again until he got it right. "How did he get to be where he is?" says his wife, Mickie, who shares his innocent steeliness. "He just worked at it. Yeah, it's a cliché. But there are so few people who are real clichés."

It's an article of faith with Krzyzewski that failure and success are connected like cause and effect. "That's why losing at the Final Four has never been a bother to me," he says. "There was a bigger thing there. It's because we reacted the way we did after we lost that we came back." . . .

THE NET result of Krzyzewski's ability to learn from defeat was a national championship in 1991, a year after Duke was routed by UNLV in the title game.

1958 | KENTUCKY'S CHEERLEADERS experienced the agony of victory as the Wildcats beat Temple in a nail-biter in the Final Four semifinals. | *Photograph by* JOHN G. ZIMMERMAN

2009 | **FLAT-OUT DISAPPOINTMENT** was what Indiana's Bobby Capobianco felt after failing to draw a charge on Kentucky's Darnell Dodson. | *Photograph by* ANDREW HANCOCK

scoring as a senior. | *Photograph by* RICH CLARKSON

2004 | ALL THAT Nigel Dixon had to show for his rim-wrecking dunk was a technical foul, a lacerated hand and, ultimately, a loss to Arkansas State. | *Photograph by* DAVID STOUT

1996 | DARVIN HAM was a smashing success for Texas Tech as he brought down the rim—and the house—in an NCAA tournament rout of North Carolina. | *Photograph by* JOEL RICHARDSON

THE COLLEGE BASKETBALL BOOK

EAST OF NAPLES, IN THE mountains, in the province of Avellino, sit two small villages. One of them is so small, in fact, that it is almost impossible to find, hidden as it is in the Calore valley, surrounded by vineyards, watched over by its patron saint, San Marciano. It is called Taurasi.

Forty years ago a five-year-old named Mario Taurasi left the hamlet of his name. His parents took him to Argentina, where he grew up, and then, in 1980, he took his wife to California. Their daughter, Diana Lurena, was born shortly thereafter, and a few years later, in the fourth grade, she took up basketball. It was immediately apparent that the kid had a facility for the game.

About 30 miles from Taurasi, east of Vesuvius, up in the Picentini range, is the town of Montella. At its highest point is the Holy Saviour, sister church to one of the same name in Norristown, Pa., a working-class suburb of Philadelphia. One day in November 1961 Marsiella Auriemma and her three children left for Norristown, where her husband, Donato, was already settled, laboring in a candy factory for 15 to 20 bucks a week. Their oldest child, Luigi, called Geno, was seven. The ride to the port in Naples was the first time he had been in a car. He had never had so much as a coin in his pocket. He could not speak a word of English.

In Norristown, at St. Francis parochial school, the nun who taught second grade explained to Geno, through an interpreter, the way things worked there. At the end of the school year, she said, the boys who passed went on to third grade. Those who didn't stayed back in second. There would be no remedial help. Pick it up on your own.

In June little Geno went up to third grade. It was obvious right off that, in any language, the kid had a way with words.

Geno grew up slick and ambitious, driven as much to chase down the big time as to outrun the nebulous fears that dogged him. "I'm the oldest, immigrant family, couldn't speak English," he says. "I'm Italian, Catholic—hey, that's enough guilt. What more do you need? I felt inferior. I grew up scared of everybody."

perfect head of swept-back curly hair: Finally, we know what became of Frankie Avalon after *Beach Blanket Bingo*. Come on, this cocksure, suave little s.o.b. is running scared?

"The worst fear of all is fear of failure," Geno says. "The year Jen Rizzotti was a sophomore, she was a chem-bio major, and she had to get a four-oh. *Had to.* I asked her one day what drove her. I hate to lose, she said. Well, then, I told her, you're my point guard, so we'll get to the final eight, maybe the Final Four, but we'll never win till you replace that *I hate to lose* with *I wanna win*. And eventually Jen did, and then we won." He pauses. "But me, I'm still motivated by fear of failure." Because you've got no coach who can change that in you? "Yeah. That's right."

Diana is harder to read. She actually looks very much like that other famous inscrutable Italian lady, Mona Lisa. When she first got to Storrs, "I called her Eddie Haskell," Geno says. "Everything was, 'No problem.' Everything was a lark."

Her freshman year the Huskies had the whole 2000 championship starting lineup back, but late in the season two All-Americas, Shea Ralph and Svetlana Abrosimova, went out with injuries. "D just decides that she's going to take on both of their roles," Geno says. "Now remember, she's a freshman. She hadn't even started at the beginning of the season. But she does it." Geno ran isolation plays, clearing out for Diana. She was the Most Outstanding Player of the NCAA East Regional.

Then, against Notre Dame, in the semis of the Final Four, disaster struck. The other Huskies were hot, but Diana was ice-cold. The freshman kept getting open, though, kept taking good shots . . . and kept missing. Notre Dame came back from 15 down in the second half to win going away. Diana made only one basket; she missed 14 shots, and when she fouled out, for once even Ms. Mona Lisa couldn't hold back the tears. Geno tried to console her. "Hey, man, relax," he said, grabbing her as she fled down the bench. "We wouldn't be here if it wasn't for you."

Amazingly, the terrible performance didn't haunt Diana. She'll even joke about it to bolster a teammate who has a bad game. "That's nothing," she'll say. "I shot 1 for 15 in the Final Four."

"See," Geno explains, "in her mind it never happened. D lives in the moment more than anybody I've ever seen. The past is gone, and there is no future. It is only right now." . . .

UNDER AURIEMMA'S watchful eye, Taurasi suffered a memorable flameout in her freshman year and then came back to win three consecutive national titles.

1955 | THE OLD Madison Square Garden didn't intimidate Hot Rod Hundley, who dropped 38 on NYU in his first visit there as a West Virginia sophomore. | *Photograph by* HY PESKIN

1962 | BOWLING GREEN was in good hands with center Nate Thurmond, who averaged 17.8 points and 17.0 boards over three seasons. | *Photograph courtesy of* BOWLING GREEN STATE UNIVERSITY

2009 | NOTRE DAME forward Zach Hillesland couldn't see the forest for the knees as he desperately passed out of a double team in a loss to UConn. | *Photograph by* MATT CASHORE

A MOTHER AND CHILD REUNION

BY S.L. PRICE

When Dwyane Wade was named SI's Sportsman of the Year in 2006, it was an opportunity to look back at one of the most dramatic moments of his life—a key game during his college career at Marquette. —*from* SI, DECEMBER 11, 2006

A BIT BEFORE NOON ON March 8, 2003, Dwyane Wade walked onto the court at Milwaukee's Bradley Center for warmups, the din of a sellout crowd beginning to rise. He had never been more nervous. He had never felt such a need to play perfectly. This wasn't because Wade, a Marquette junior about to skip his senior year for the NBA draft, knew it would be his final collegiate home game. It wasn't because he had the chance to lead the school to its first Conference USA title with a victory over perennial champion Cincinnati. Just three days earlier Wade's mother had been released from a maximum-security prison in Dwight, Ill., after serving time for a drug conviction. Jolinda had attended only two of Dwyane's games, early in high school. This would be his first chance to show her what he had become.

Dwyane, who hadn't seen his mom in nearly 16 months, kept stealing looks into the stands. Jolinda had come up with her daughter, Tragil, that morning from Chicago, after getting permission from her parole officer to leave the state, but Dwyane hadn't dared talk to her before the game, afraid an emotional overload would leave him sapped. Everything in his life had pointed to this moment; when Dwyane was born his mother had heard a word, *blessing*, in her head, and she had wanted that to be his name: Blessing Wade. He was glad it wasn't, but he tried to live up to it. Throughout high school, during three years at Marquette, Wade drove himself to exhaustion, believing if he could only break out big, be that kid who rose from welfare, he could save her. Almost daily, over the last year, they had written to each other. "If anybody's going to give you inspiration," Dwyane wrote, "it's going to be me. I'm going to show you that you can overcome too."

It had taken a while. During Dwyane's freshman year, in 2000–01, he was forced to sit out the season because he had fallen a point short on his ACT exam. But during that year he beefed up his skinny frame in the weight room and learned how to better see and work the floor. And over the Christmas break he proposed to his girlfriend, Siohvaughn. By the following spring they were married and she was pregnant. Wade was 20, and determined not to give his child the life that he'd had.

Back in Chicago, though, Jolinda was still using. In 1996 she had violated the terms of a work-release program and there was an arrest warrant out in her name. She lived as a fugitive from the law until finally, on Oct. 14, 2001, during Dwyane's sophomore year, she sat in church and felt the hypocrite's shame. She called a friend, who drove her to a house in South Bend, where, without methadone, with nothing but prayer and isolation, Jolinda sweated and got sick, and eventually, clean. Then, in December that year, she met with Dwyane at a church kitchen and told him the good news—and the bad. She said she was sober, but if she wanted to be a true mother to him and a grandmother to the baby to come, she had to turn herself in.

On New Year's Eve, 2001, Jolinda presented herself to the Chicago police and returned to prison to serve out her sentence. For the next year and two months, while Dwyane was becoming a father to a son, Zaire, and getting married and becoming a basketball revelation, while he was leading Marquette through a 2002–03 season that would result in a 23–4 record and the school's first Final Four appearance in 26 years, the star's mother counted her days in prison. Jolinda read Dwyane's letters and felt stronger, but being locked up had left her rehabilitation unfinished. Once freed, she would have every opportunity to use again.

But there was something powerful about that Cincinnati game. For Dwyane, to have his mother, his sister, his wife and his son together for the first time, watching him win his first championship, filled him with a sensation he'd never known. To see Jolinda, to see them all, cheering him? "It's what life is about," Wade says. For Jolinda, seeing Dwyane play the hero—26 points, 10 rebounds, making big plays, holding up his No. 1 finger at the end—felt like a dream. The Milwaukee crowd chanted "Wade! Wade!"—still her name too—and lifted him off the court when the game was over. Mother and son locked eyes, and she heard a voice in her head: *Here comes another chance now, Jolinda. A chance to be a mother to your son. . . .*

WADE JOINED the pros after his junior season, in 2003, but not before leading Marquette to its first Final Four appearance in 26 years.

1997 | LOOKING BACK on 36 years as North Carolina's coach, Dean Smith counted two titles, 11 Final Fours and SI's Sportsman of the Year award in his legacy. | *Photograph by* BRIAN LANKER

1951 | FUNDAMENTALLY SOUND right from the start, Smith won his first championship as a reserve guard on the '52 Kansas title team. | *Photograph by* RICH CLARKSON

2006 | A SEMINOLE MOMENT for Florida State fans came as their team knocked off No. 1–ranked Duke, sparking a mad dash onto the court. | *Photograph by* JIMMY DEFLIPPO

THE
1990s

1991 | HE WAS more J. Crew than 2 Live Crew, but Duke center Christian Laettner could be nasty when he had to be while leading the Blue Devils to four Final Fours and two national championships. | *Photograph by* PETER READ MILLER

F - ARKANSAS

Larry Johnson
F - UNLV

Christian Laettner
C - DUKE

WOMEN

Dawn Staley
G - VIRGINA

Jennifer Rizzotti
G - CONNECTICUT

Chamique Holdsclaw
F - TENNESSEE

Sheryl Swoopes
F - TEXAS TECH

Rebecca Lobo
C - CONNECTICUT

to the Rebels showed up the following season. Michigan's Fab Five was surely an aggregation made for the video age, which unofficially began on March 3, 1991, when an amateur photographer captured the beating of motorist Rodney King by several Los Angeles policemen.

The old order was under fire everywhere. In South Africa, Nelson Mandela was released in February of 1990 after 27 years in prison, and in Eastern Europe, country after country declared independence from the Soviet Union. Magic Johnson shocked the world in '91 by quitting the NBA because he was HIV-positive, and, three years later, a popular former running back took off in a white Bronco.

But the Old Guard came storming back in college hoops. Duke got its revenge on UNLV in '91 and beat back the Fab Five to repeat in '92. And for the rest of the decade, which ended with a former pro wrestler (Jesse Ventura) getting elected governor of Minnesota and a sitting President (Bill Clinton) claiming that he "did not have sexual relations with that woman," the college crown was claimed by traditional powers. —J.M.

O.J. Simpson's trial fixated the nation in '95.

NATIONAL CHAMPION		COACH
'90*	**UNLV**	Jerry Tarkanian
'91	**DUKE**	Mike Krzyzewski
'92	**DUKE**	Mike Krzyzewski
'93	**NORTH CAROLINA**	Dean Smith
'94	**ARKANSAS**	Nolan Richardson
'95	**UCLA**	Jim Harrick
'96	**KENTUCKY**	Rick Pitino
'97	**ARIZONA**	Lute Olson
'98	**KENTUCKY**	Tubby Smith
'99	**CONNECTICUT**	Jim Calhoun

* DENOTES YEAR IN WHICH SEASON ENDED

LEADING SCORER	POINTS PER GAME
BO KIMBLE, Loyola Marymount	35.3
KEVIN BRADSHAW, U.S. International	37.6
BRETT ROBERTS, Morehead State	28.1
GREG GUY, Texas-Pan American	29.3
GLENN ROBINSON, Purdue	30.3
KURT THOMAS, TCU	28.9
KEVIN GRANGER, Texas Southern	27.0
CHARLES JONES, LIU	30.1
CHARLES JONES, LIU	29.0
ALVIN YOUNG, Niagara	25.1

LEADING REBOUNDER	REBOUNDS PER GAME
ANTHONY BONNER, Saint Louis	13.8
SHAQUILLE O'NEAL, LSU	14.7
POPEYE JONES, Murray State	14.4
WARREN KIDD, Middle Tennessee State	14.8
JEROME LAMBERT, Baylor	14.8
KURT THOMAS, TCU	14.6
MARCUS MANN, Mississippi Valley State	13.6
TIM DUNCAN, Wake Forest	14.7
RYAN PERRYMAN, Dayton	12.5
IAN McGINNIS, Dartmouth	12.2

>> WISH YOU WERE THERE

Duke 104, Kentucky 103 (OT) >

MARCH 28, 1992 • THE SPECTRUM, PHILADELPHIA
Christian Laettner (*right*) completes a perfect East Regional final (10 of 10 from the field and 10 of 10 from the line) by making the college game's most memorable buzzerbeater. With Duke down a point and :02.1 left in OT, the tournament's alltime leading scorer catches a three-quarters-court inbounds pass from Grant Hill, turns and hits a 15-foot jumper over Kentucky's Deron Feldhaus to get the Blue Devils to the Final Four.

North Carolina 77, Michigan 71

APRIL 5, 1993 • LOUISIANA SUPERDOME, NEW ORLEANS
Trailing 73–71 with :11 left, Michigan's Chris Webber grabs a missed Tar Heel free throw and, instead of getting the ball to a guard, dribbles to the frontcourt and calls timeout. Unfortunately, Michigan has none remaining and is hit with a T. The Heels' Donald Williams makes the free throws to ice Carolina's title.

Arkansas 76, Duke 72

APRIL 4, 1994 • CHARLOTTE COLISEUM, CHARLOTTE Bill Clinton, the first sitting President to attend a Final Four, watches his Razorbacks

storm back from a 48–38 second-half deficit as Corliss Williamson scores a gamehigh 23 points and Scotty Thurman sinks a clutch three-pointer in the final minute to give Arkansas its first national title.

UCLA 75, Missouri 74

MARCH 19, 1995 • BSU PAVILION, BOISE, IDAHO
With top-seeded UCLA down one with 4.8 seconds left, guard Tyus Edney takes the inbounds pass, eludes a midcourt defender with a behind-the-back dribble and floats the game-winner over 6' 9" Derek Grimm to allow the eventual tournament champs to move on to the Sweet 16.

Stanford 79, Rhode Island 77

MARCH 22, 1998 • KIEL CENTER, ST. LOUIS
Cardinal point guard Arthur Lee scores 13 of his game-high 26 points in the final 2:04, then makes a crucial steal to set up Mark Madsen for the go-ahead three-point play and a 76–74 lead with 32 ticks left as Stanford advances to its first Final Four since 1942. With the score 77–74, Rams' point guard Tyson Wheeler, who scored 24 points in the game, misses three straight free throws that could have tied the game at 77 all with five seconds remaining.

GAME CHANGER
PETE CARRIL
THE PRINCETON OFFENSE

The gnomish Carril wore out Tigers foes with an oh-so-deliberate attack based on passing and screening. Its coup de grace is the backdoor play, a hard cut to the hoop when a defender (*in blue*) overplays a pass, as illustrated in the diagram at right by the movement of the small forward (*3, red*). The threat of the backdoor cut, in turn, can cause defenders to sag toward the basket (*middle*), allowing offensive players to pop out for an open shot on the wing.

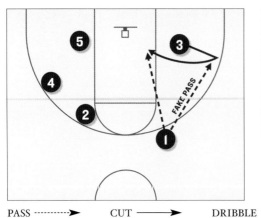
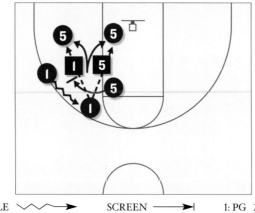
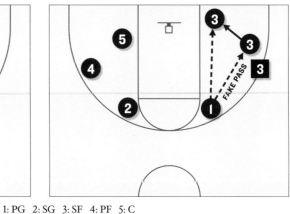

PASS --------->   CUT ———>   DRIBBLE ∿∿∿→   SCREEN ———⊢   1: PG 2: SG 3: SF 4: PF 5: C

badass enough to stomp Kentucky's Aminu Timberlake on the chest in the '92 East Regional final in retaliation for being pushed to the floor earlier.

THE WOMAN In four seasons at Tennessee, Chamique Holdsclaw led the Lady Vols to a 131–17 record, including the first 39–0 season in NCAA history. But her star burned brightest in the NCAAs. She is still the tournament's alltime leading scorer, and with her leading the way, the Lady Vols became the first women's team to win three consecutive national championships, in '96, '97 and '98.

deliberate offense, Princeton did have the eighth-best record (210–66, .761) in Division I in the '90s.

THE CINDERELLA After the death of forward Hank Gathers, who collapsed and died during the West Coast Conference tournament, 11th seeded Loyola Marymount reached the 1990 Elite Eight before falling to eventual champ UNLV. The highlight came in the second round as the Lions upset third-seeded Michigan 149–115—still a record for the most points scored in a tournament game.

Decals made their mark at Arkansas in '94.

the most points scored against a Division I team. The Gulls, though, allowed the most points in D-I history, losing 186–140.

16 | Seed of the Harvard women's team which beat top-seeded Stanford 71–67 at Maples Pavilion, the Cardinal home court, on March 14, 1998.

2 | Consecutive games in which Oklahoma defeated the No. 1 team in the nation. On Feb. 25, 1990 the Sooners beat Missouri 107–90 and two days later topped new No. 1 Kansas, 100–78.

8.37 | Career assists per game by N.C. State point guard Chris Corchiani, highest ever by a four-year player.

BASKETBALL BABYLON
TARNISHED GOPHERS

Just as the 1999 NCAA tournament was set to start, four Minnesota players were suspended after former tutor Jan Gangelhoff told NCAA officials that she completed at least 400 items of course work for as many as 20 Minnesota basketball players from 1993 through '98. Coach Clem Haskins (*left*) initially denied any knowledge of the academic fraud, but the following June he took a $1.5 million buyout. (He was later forced to return it.) An investigation also found that Haskins advised his players to lie to school officials, and he was barred from coaching for seven years and the school was stripped of all basketball records from '93 through '99.

$1.725 | Value in *billions* of the 1994 CBS contract to broadcast the tournament through 2002.

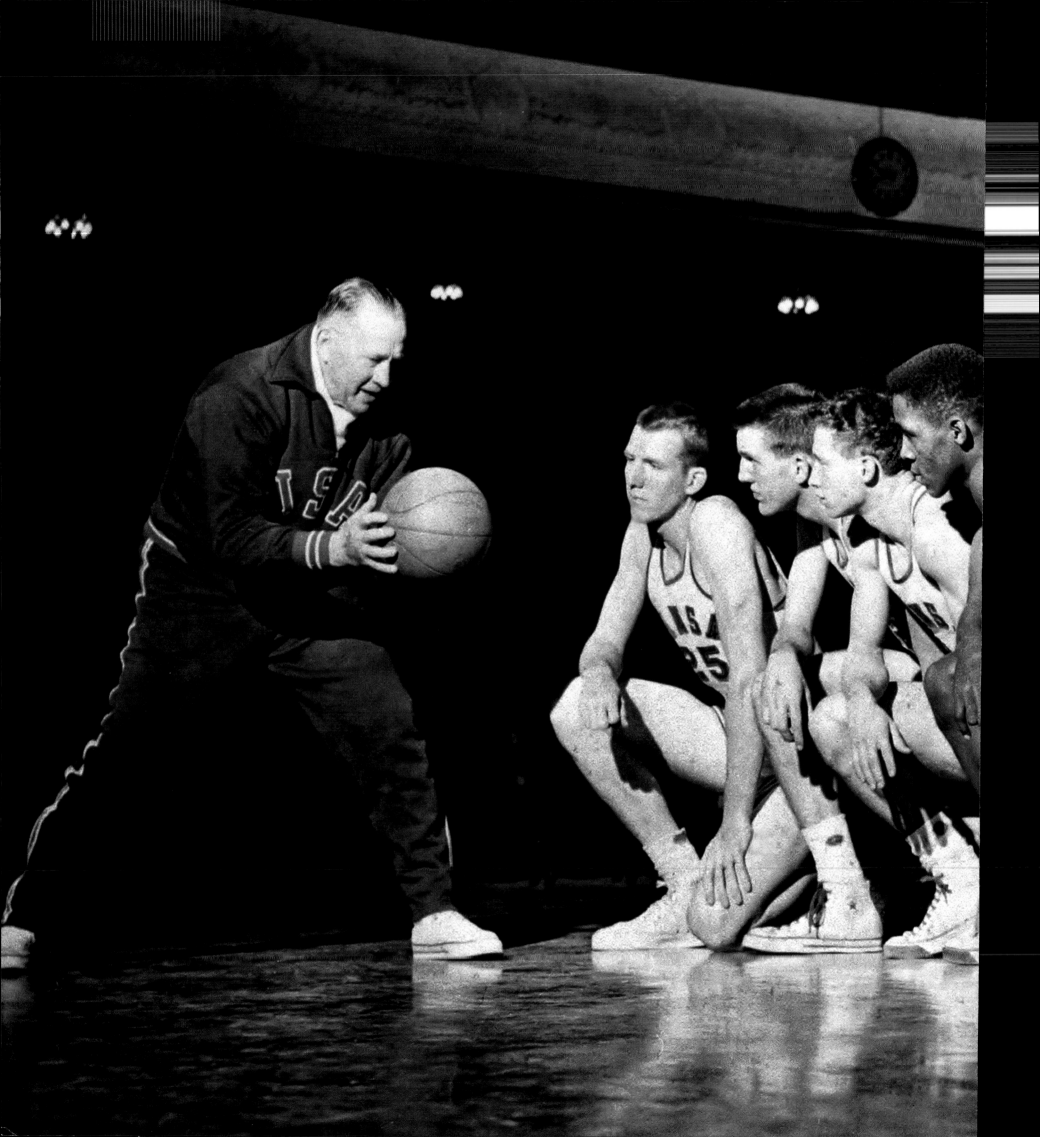

HOW KING RAT BECAME BIG CHEESE

BY CURRY KIRKPATRICK

N.C. State's coach Jim Valvano was one of the game's great originals, and his death from cancer at age 47 was a terrible loss, but this profile in the months after his team's stunning upset of Houston in the 1983 championship game is a reminder of the great vitality with which he lived. —*from* SI, DECEMBER 5, 1983

Y EAH, WELL, ALL THE STORIES about V are four-fifths quotes anyway, and since V is tired and hungry and his throat's scratchy and he says he's injured because he pulled a muscle in his tongue, the magazine guy figured he'd begin the story by trying to write the way V talks—without the f's, of course. No question. *No question about it.*

Take his national championship ... please. No, really. About the look-alike stuff, V says it's O.K. It's fine. It's great. Of course he loves it. No question. When V started out as Namath, he says they looked at Namath and said he was ruggedly handsome, but they looked at V and said he had a big nose. Then V was Pacino—son of Godfather, *Godfather III* and all that—which was O.K. because that meant he was probably Hoffman too, so he started signing autographs "Love, Tootsie," and he loved every minute of it, but then they called him Ratso Rizzo, and V didn't think that was so hot. V didn't like Ratso Rizzo at all, because how many broads want to talk to Ratso? No question about it. Zero. V wasn't no Ratso. But wait a minute. That's another paradox, because all his life V has said there were only two kinds of people: Big-timers and Rats. And V was the Rat of all Rats. So what was so different?

Big-timers are celebrities, rich and famous, powerful and full of themselves. The kind of guys who fly in from the Coast to the summer camps and don't do right by the kids. Question-and-answer artists who do 10 minutes and split for the cocktail lounge. Phonies and frauds and guys who forget where they came from.

Rats are the little people, the blue-collar guys, the workers who struggle and overcome. The world needs Rats because Rats play the great D and get in people's jocks and shuffle-cut

to breakfast and double-team a tree. And, yeah, Rats take the charge. Absolutely. No question about it.

Didn't V give out RAT shirts and make up Rat slogans and carry a stuffed Rat mounted on a skateboard to all those 90 camps that summer and keep that stuffed Rat in his office until his wife finally threw it out? Didn't V say he still was one full-fledged amazing Rat right up to and including that night last April in Albuquerque, where in the locker room before the final NCAA tournament game he ranted and raved and got down smack in their faces and, growling from deep within those sandpaper lungs, challenged every last one of those other Rats?

You, Lowe, you are going to go out and handle and dish and play the game of your life and lead us to the national championship! And you, Whitt, you are going to take those downtown Js and shoot the lights out and play the game of your life and lead us to the national championship! And you, Bailey, you are going to jump and bang and control the rock and play the game of your life and lead us to the national championship! *No question.*

And didn't V challenge himself, the King Rat of Rats, by telling them: Me? V? I'm ready. I've never been so ready. I'm 37 years old and I've been dreaming of this moment all my life and preparing for it maybe longer than that. Me? I'm going to go out there and X and O and think and scream and coach the living hell out of this game, and we are going to win the national championship. And when V did just that; when Rocco and Angelina's kid from Alstyne Avenue in Corona, Queens, coached the living hell out of the NCAA title game and won that sucker for the Wolfpack, didn't V complain that from then on his most difficult struggle would be to keep from being a Big-timer and remain a Rat?

Ratso Rizzo? Of course V is Ratso. And thank goodness for that, because, as another older, more Westernized Rat, name of John Wooden, wrote in a letter to V following the season, "Your effort in the tournament this year and that of Don Haskins in 1966 are the two finest NCAA tournament coaching jobs I have ever seen. You are great for the profession . . . please do not change." There was no question about it. . . .

ON THE biggest stage of his career, Valvano pulled off one of the greatest performances in coaching history, and he had the good grace to enjoy every second of it.

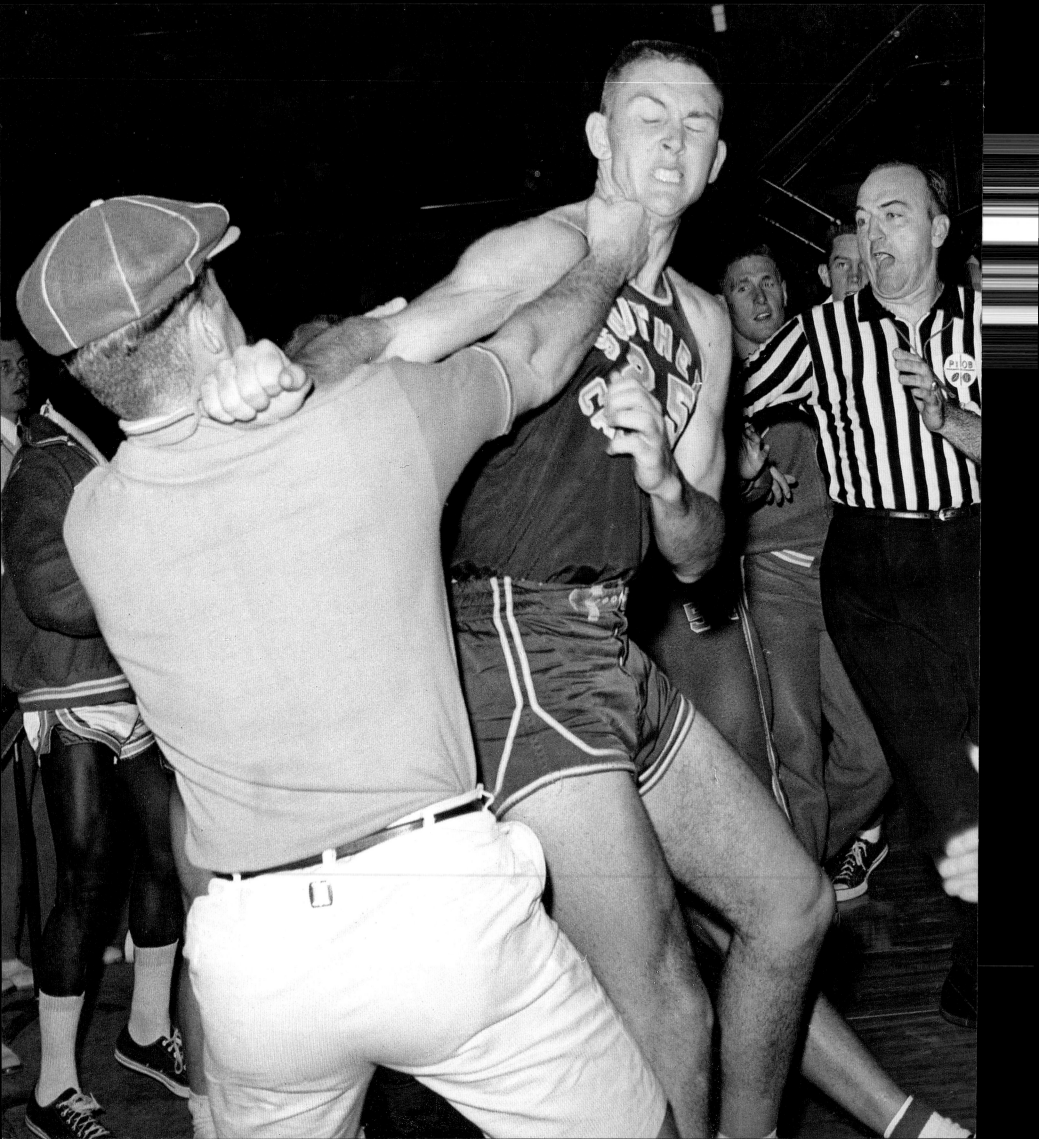

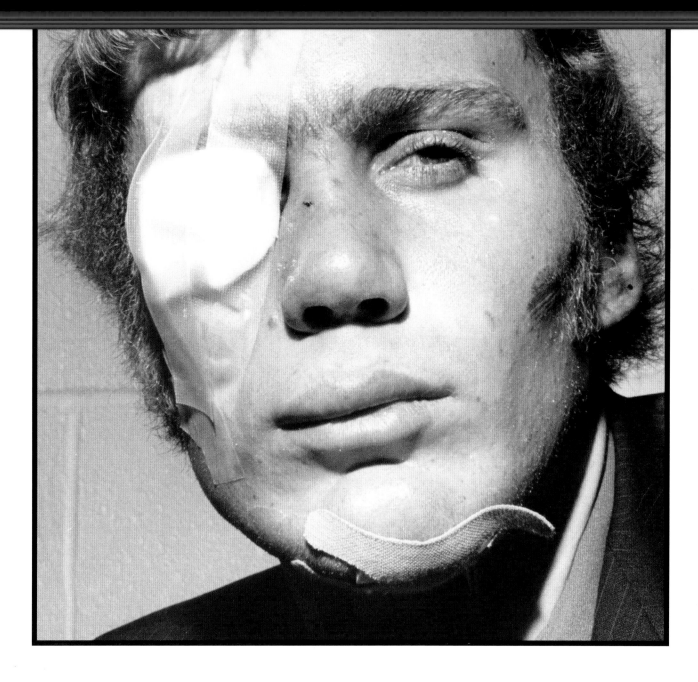

1972 | THE BATTERED face of Ohio State's Luke Witte was testament to one of the game's darkest moments, a brutal stomping he took at Minnesota. | *Photograph by* DICK GARRETT

1960 | FAN INVOLVEMENT is a plus, until it goes too far, as when USC's Ken Stanley brawled with a UCLA supporter en route to a bitter Trojan loss. | *Photograph by* BETTMANN/CORBIS

1983 | LARRY MICHEAUX (40) was the man in the middle as Houston's Phi Slamma Jamma frat outbattled Louisville in the NCAA semifinals. | *Photograph by* RICH CLARKSON

2007 | TYLER HANSBROUGH (50) wore out the paint at North Carolina, leaving school as the Heels' alltime No. 1 scorer and rebounder. | *Photograph by* GREG NELSON

I T IS QUITE POSSIBLE THAT, AFTER all these years, Cheryl Miller has become less a phenomenon on a basketball court, where she is surrounded by women of similar size, proportions, age and sweaty grunginess, than off one. This has to do not so much with her 6' 3" height—Miller suggests she is closer to 6' 2" but, unlike the boys, the girls always cheat down—which is nonetheless striking in civilian life, as it does with a personality, a look and bearing, a commanding presence that Miller seems able to adjust chameleonlike, according to the situation. She is the world, she is the children. Do cute, Cheryl. Or do vamp. And it's done. Miller can charm a Senate hearing with learned testimony on behalf of the Civil Rights Act of 1984 just as easily as she can get down and dirty with some in-your-face street talk.

With apologies to Wayne Gretzky, Miller probably is the most dominating individual in a team sport of this era. Arguably she is the finest basketball player of her gender who ever lived. Miller's goal this final season is to play so spectacularly well that, as she says, "You can strike *arguably*" from that phrase. Fellow 1984 Olympian Kim Mulkey, now an assistant coach at Louisiana Tech, says simply, "Women's basketball *is* Cheryl Miller." And beyond this: What athletes transcend their sport? How many transcend while still playing? Ruth, perhaps. Ali, maybe. Jackie Robinson. And now a 21-year-old black-magic woman and dyna-kid princess from down the lane in Riverside, Calif.

Before Miller was out of high school she had blithely scattered legacies in her wake as if they were pocketsful of posies. She was—and is and ever will be—excitement, intensity, flamboyance. She is the Follow-through Hotdog Wrist. She is the on-court cartwheel. She is—for goodness sakes—a *haircut*. Little girls all over the basketball yards of California now come turned out in "Cheryl Miller" 'dos. Miller's own younger brother, UCLA's estimable 6' 7" junior forward Reggie, the most valuable player in last year's NIT, is a budding star in his own right. But on the road he is yet a haunted creature of disdain for opposing crowds who wail "Cher-yl, Cher-yl" at the poor fellow whenever he steps to the foul line. In the

High in Riverside. Poly's 84-game winning streak. The two NCAA championship teams at USC. The electrifying Grammy awards cameo appearance during *She Works Hard for the Money*—Donna Summer is still wondering what hit her. The Olympic gold medal. Magazine covers in Japan and India. The BBC on hold. Chats with Ronald Reagan, not to mention Cagney and Lacey. A *Face the Nation* guest shot. Kissy-kissy with Barbara Walters. *Rick Dees!*

Cheryl Miller? Is that Cheryl Miller still around?

Just as the Los Angeles Olympics surely aroused interest in the women's game, so have Miller's yeowoman individual efforts. Her captivating interpretive style has taken the sport to another level and added visibility and drawing power both locally and on the national scene. In Miller's freshman season the Women of Troy broke 11 attendance records on the road and sold out four home dates. Since then the team has had to abandon the small campus gym and schedule its home games in the Los Angeles Sports Arena and elsewhere.

Miller has been fortunate in that her arrival in the big time coincided with a combination of powerful forces such as the positive effects of Title IX, the greater attention shown women athletes by the media and the growth of the feminist movement. No such forces existed back when Nera White was burning up the AAU nets for Nashville Business College in the 1960s. In that era of the six-woman teams (inclusive of twin "rovers" and the three-dribble rule), White was a multi-year All-America. Theresa Shank of Immaculata and Lucy Harris of Delta State, each of whom led her team to three national championships in the 1970s, were the next female superstars. Carol (the Blaze) Blazejowski of Rutgers, Ann Meyers of UCLA, Nancy Lieberman of Old Dominion and Lynette Woodard of Kansas followed them, talented maids all in a layup row.

But Miller's edge is her totality, the fact that she excels in all the phases. "Cheryl has revolutionized the game," says Lieberman. "She's taught young girls to play hard all the time and to be physical. The flamboyance is her bread and butter. She sees those cameras and she seizes the moment. Sure, it's all Hollywood, but that's O.K., too. I think Cheryl is the best thing that could have happened to the game." . . .

STILL THE sixth-leading women's scorer *and* rebounder alltime, Miller won three Player of the Year awards and two national titles at USC.

2011 | BUTLER CRASHED two straight title games with tough D like the sandwich Matt Howard (54) and Chrishawn Hopkins (20) made of Florida's Erving Walker. | *Photograph by* KEVIN C. COX

2011 | VIRGINIA COMMONWEALTH got uncommonly good playmaking from Joey Rodriguez in a rout of Purdue on the way to the Rams' first Final Four. | *Photograph by* JOHN BIEVER

The Birth Of a Legend

From the first glimpse of his recruiting file, big things were expected of Michael Jordan at North Carolina, and he didn't let anyone down

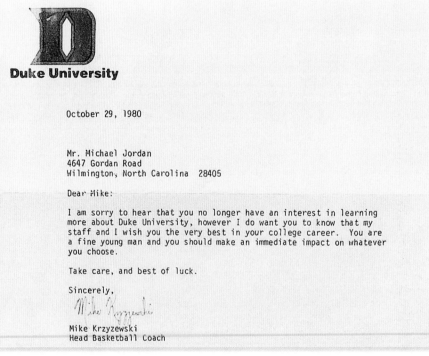

12/22/79
Please check with Coach Clifton Herring at Laney High School, New Hanover County

Re: MICHAEL JORDAN, 6'4" junior, averaging 25 points per game; yet "unknown," but likened by his Jayvee coach to Walter Davis

Eddie — Give courtesy copy to Roland Gidez CH Newspaper (He oky this)

Dean Smith noted Jordan as a high schooler to watch in '79.

Dancing in the dorm in '83.

Duke University

October 29, 1980

Mr. Michael Jordan
4647 Gordan Road
Wilmington, North Carolina 28405

Dear Mike:

I am sorry to hear that you no longer have an interest in learning more about Duke University, however I do want you to know that my staff and I wish you the very best in your college career. You are a fine young man and you should make an immediate impact on whatever you choose.

Take care, and best of luck.

Sincerely,

Mike Krzyzewski
Head Basketball Coach

Mike Krzyzewski reacted to the bad news that Jordan wouldn't be attending Duke.

1982 | JORDAN FINISHED off Georgetown and his freshman year with a bang, hitting the Final game winner and then clipping the net. | *Photograph by* BRIAN SMITH

1958 | IN REPOSE, Cincinnati's Oscar Robertson could look almost statuesque, but in action he was unstoppable. | *Photograph by* COLLEGIATE IMAGES

FAST AND FURIOUS

BY GRANT WAHL

During his coaching tenure at Memphis, John Calipari totally reinvented his offensive approach to the game, and his unlikely mentor was a junior college coach few people had ever heard of

—*from* SI, FEBRUARY 18, 2008

WHEN HOOPS HISTORIANS look back on the 2007–08 college basketball season, they may conclude that its most significant moment came on an Indian summer evening in October '03. At the head of a heavy oak table in his Memphis steak house sat Tigers coach John Calipari, who has led teams to both the Final Four and the NBA playoffs. Next to him was an obscure junior college coach from Fresno named Vance Walberg. For six days Walberg had observed Calipari's practices, continuing an annual pilgrimage that had given him deeper insight into the work of two dozen elite college coaches, from Bob Knight to Dean Smith to Billy Donovan.

But now, after the remnants of the porterhouses had been cleared from the table, Calipari asked Walberg something that no other coach had bothered to ask him. "So tell me, Vance," he said, "what do you run?"

Walberg laughed. "You don't want to know," he replied. "It's a little bit off the wall."

"No, really," Calipari said. "Show me."

And so, using a pepper shaker as the basket, white sugar packets as offensive players and pink Sweet'N Low packets as defenders, Walberg explained his quirky creation, a high-scoring scheme featuring four perimeter players and a host of innovations. Unlike Knight's classic motion offense (which is based on screens) or Pete Carril's Princeton offense (which is based on cuts), Walberg's attack was founded on dribble penetration. To Calipari, at least, it embodied two wholly unconventional notions. One, there were no screens, the better to create spacing for drives. Two, the post man ran to the weak side of the lane (instead of the ball side), leaving the ball handler an open driving path to the basket. As Walberg pushed the packets through the phases of his offense, Calipari experienced a new kind of sugar rush. Walberg's scheme was genius.

And it was unlike anything Calipari, an old school motion-and-play-calling analyst, had ever run. "The players are unleashed when they play this way," he says, "because every player has the green light to take his man on every play." When Calipari junked his playbook and switched to Walberg's offense, his mentors thought he had lost his mind. "You've won hundreds of games playing a certain way, and now you're going to change?" Hall of Famer Larry Brown asked him. "And it's a junior college coach from California? What are you, crazy?"

Now look. Through Sunday, Calipari's Tigers were 23–0, ranked No. 1 in the nation and aiming to become the first team to enter the NCAA tournament undefeated since UNLV in 1991. But Memphis is only the tip of the Walberg iceberg, a spreading mass of teams using the Dribble-Drive Motion offense—Calipari's felicitous term—at every level of the game.

In Jersey City legendary coach Bob Hurley, who adopted DDM two seasons ago, has taken St. Anthony (19–0) to No. 1 in *USA Today*'s national high school rankings. The Denver Nuggets are running elements of DDM, and so are the Boston Celtics. "[Calipari] and I fax each other," says Celtics coach Doc Rivers.

As a high school grinder for many years—he even coached badminton at one point—Walberg dabbled in variations of the flex offense and Knight's motion, among other schemes, but his real break came in 1997, at Clovis West High.

"It was pure luck," Walberg says, despite all evidence to the contrary. His best player, a heady, relentless point guard named Chris Hernandez (who would later star at Stanford), was such a skilled dribble-penetrator that Walberg moved his post man to the weakside block, clearing two bodies from Hernandez's path to the basket. When Hernandez broke down his defender he had several options: 1) shoot an open layup, 2) pass to the post man (if the post defender left him to stop Hernandez), or 3) kick the ball out to an open teammate on the perimeter (if a defender had sagged inside to help out on Hernandez). The open player could shoot a three pointer, but if one wasn't available, the team would attack again.

Because there were no screens and because attackers were spaced so far apart, the formation opened yawning gaps for penetrators, as long as the players had the talent to beat their defenders and the smarts to read defenses on the fly. "I wanted kids to understand that it was attack-attack-skip-attack-attack," says Walberg. "What am I trying to say? Get to the rim. It's basically here we come." . . .

BY STATIONING his post player on the weak side (lower right) rather than the strong side, Calipari opened up driving lanes that his slashing stars could exploit.

1993 | ED O'BANNON was a slam-dunk Player of the Year as a senior after leading UCLA to its first title in 20 seasons in '95. | *Photograph by* RICHARD MACKSON

1968 | WIELDING HIS rolled-up program like a scepter, John Wooden ruled the college game with 10 titles in 12 years at UCLA. | *Photograph by* RICH CLARKSON

2009 | **FUTURE NBA** slam-dunk champion Blake Griffin got his start as the poster boy of posterizing at Oklahoma. | *Photograph by* GREG NELSON

2001 | **MARQUIS ESTILL** of Kentucky was a sight for sore eyes as he powered to the rim above Tennessee defender Charles Hathaway. | *Photograph by* BOB ROSATO

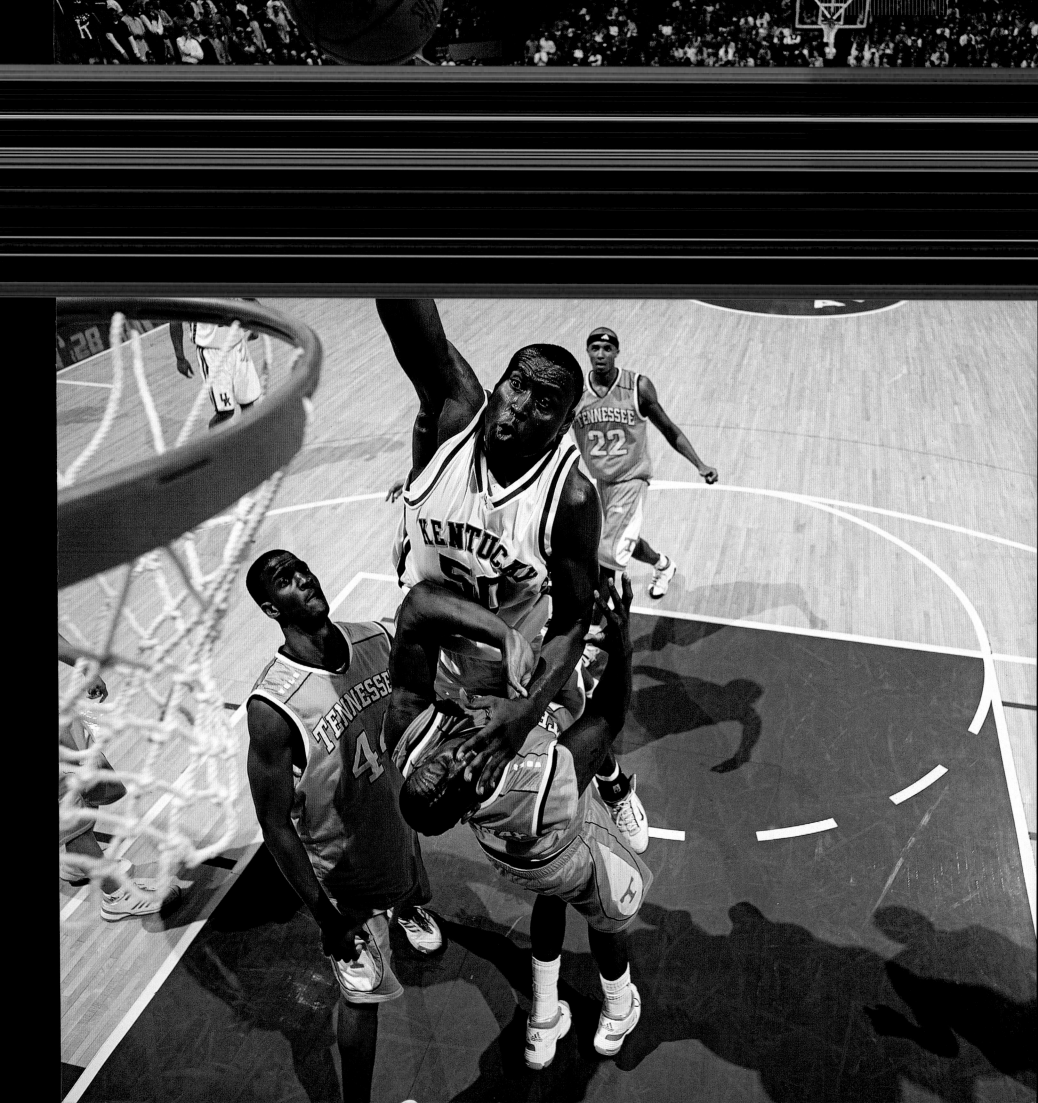

CLARENCE (BIGHOUSE) GAINES, the only child of Olivia and Lester Gaines, grew up Methodist on the banks of the Ohio River, in a city that was a way station between Chicago and the spreading South. People came through Paducah, and because his parents managed, and later owned, the Metropolitan House—nothing luxurious, but it was clean and was one of the only places between Memphis and Chicago where blacks could get room and board—Clarence had seen Marian Anderson and Ella Fitzgerald sing, and he had eaten with the bands of Chick Webb and Cab Calloway and had listened to the sidemen improvise. These were talented people. Talented people were always going somewhere else. Paducah was just a pit stop.

A star in football and basketball at Lincoln High, Gaines faced a limited choice of colleges in 1941 for reasons that had nothing to do with test scores. He ended up in Baltimore, at Morgan State, the powerhouse team of the CIAA, a grouping of 14 traditionally black colleges founded in 1912. It was there that a fellow named Jimmy Carter told him he was as big as a house, coining a nickname that remains to this day.

Four years later, bachelor's degree in hand and with some vague notion about becoming a dentist one day, Gaines gypsied down to Winston-Salem Teachers College at the recommendation of his football coach to take a job as an assistant to basketball coach Brutus Wilson. When he got there, Gaines found a school of 500 women and 75 men training to become schoolteachers. Gaines didn't plan to stay very long.

"The college was so small then," says former school president Kenneth Williams, "we hardly had intramurals. Gaines had a reputation as a football player. No one knew much about his basketball. This was supposed to be temporary. But the college discovered he had a great deal to offer. He discovered he could do something with the fellows. He began to win. That led to relationships. He set up a network of former players as recruiters up and down the East Coast."

Soon they were sending Gaines players like Jack DeFares,

The CIAA was cooking by the late '50s, and the league's coaches and their players had become legends, at least on their small campuses on their sides of small towns throughout the South. John McLendon at North Carolina College in Durham—he had Sam Jones, the future Celtic and NBA All-Star. Mark Cardwell at West Virginia State had Earl Lloyd, who would later perform with the Detroit Pistons. Virginia Union had Jumpin' Jackie Jackson. Globetrotter great Curly Neal was at Johnson C. Smith College in Charlotte. Cal Irvin, 25 miles away at North Carolina A&T in Greensboro, had Alvin Attles.

Gaines often wondered what he could have done if, say, a Wilt Chamberlain had come along. Someone like Wilt came along rarely enough. Never to Winston-Salem. Not a chance.

Then along came Cleo Hill.

"I had done just enough work to get by at South Side High," says Hill now. "I was already known as a ballplayer. Abe Saperstein had already contacted me, promising a spot on the Globetrotters. Well, they had remedial courses at Winston-Salem, and I needed them. Gaines made it known I'd have to do the work. He brought in Jim Brown to talk about education. I swore Jim was talking to me alone. So, in that kind of environment, with my kind of game, I suppose I flourished a little."

So much so that during Hill's senior season, an All-Atlantic Coast Conference playmaking guard from Bones McKinney's Wake Forest team over on the west side of Winston-Salem decided he wanted to see Hill play. It never entered the young Billy Packer's mind that he was going behind a curtain. So he came to Whitaker Gymnasium in 1960 to watch a Rams game and found himself the only white person in the arena.

"I had hitchhiked across town," says Packer, who is now CBS's principal college basketball commentator. "I wasn't even thinking about east Winston-Salem being a place where I wasn't supposed to be. I guess when you're young, you don't think that way. That was the first time I saw Bighouse. I wasn't hard to pick out. He said, 'Son, you better come sit on the bench with me.' So I did. I watched. Cleo Hill remains one of the greatest college players I've ever seen. We got the exposure in the ACC, even though Cleo was far better than I had ever thought about being. As for Bighouse, he was a great man then and still is." . . .

GAINES CAME to Winston-Salem State with no intention of sticking around and stayed for 47 years, retiring in 1993 with 828 wins, then second-most alltime.

1945 | NO-NONSENSE COACH Henry Iba won two-straight NCAA titles at Oklahoma A&M with Bob Kurland (90), the game's first great 7-footer. | *Photograph by* JOE MILLER

1976 | THE HAIR-RAISING Rebels of UNLV coach Jerry Tarkanian thumbed their noses at the usual 'dos and don'ts. | *Photograph by* HANK DELESPINASSE STUDIOS

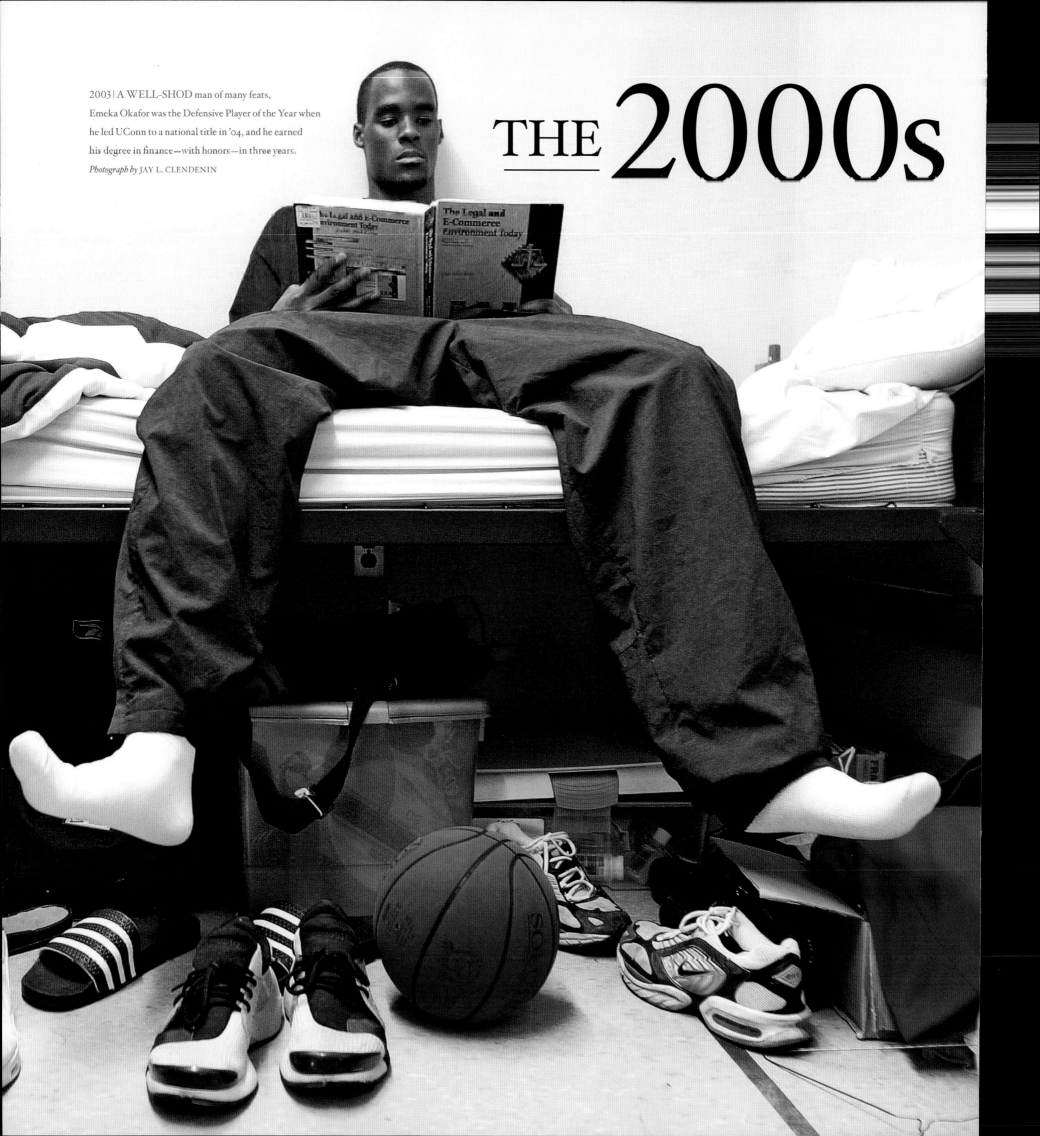

2003 | A WELL-SHOD man of many feats, Emeka Okafor was the Defensive Player of the Year when he led UConn to a national title in '04, and he earned his degree in finance—with honors—in three years.

Photograph by JAY L. CLENDENIN

THE 2000s

Phelps paddled past Mark Spitz with eight golds in Beijing in 2008); and major publications (*Harry Potter and the Deathly Hollows* sold more than 15 million copies worldwide in the first 24 hours of its release in 2007).

And in October of 2003, a little-known Harvard student changed the world in his own quiet way, launching a Web program called Facemash that, with a name change to Facebook, turned into both an engine of political change and a place for embarrassing party photos. So if a computer geek named Zuckerberg could become a billionaire almost overnight, why shouldn't the have-nots of college hoops get in on the action, too?

In 2006, little George Mason made it to the Final Four, and in 2010 Butler almost upset Duke in the NCAA tournament title game. Butler then shocked the world in '11 by returning to the Final Four—along with 11th-seeded Virginia Commonwealth! And suddenly the memory of John Wooden's UCLA dynasty, with stars such as Walt Hazzard, Gail Goodrich, Lew Alcindor and Bill Walton coming back year after year, now seems so quaint and so very long ago.   —J.M.

Mark Zuckerberg changed the world one algorithm at a time.

F - SYRACUSE

Shane Battier
F - DUKE

Tyler Hansbrough
C - NORTH CAROLINA

WOMEN

Diana Taurasi
G - CONNECTICUT

Seimone Augustus
G - LSU

Maya Moore
F - CONNECTICUT

Candace Parker
F - TENNESSEE

Tina Charles
C - CONNECTICUT

NATIONAL CHAMPION		LEADING SCORER		LEADING REBOUNDER	
	COACH		POINTS PER GAME		REBOUNDS PER GAME
'00* MICHIGAN STATE	Tom Izzo	COURTNEY ALEXANDER, Fresno State	24.8	DARREN PHILLIP, Fairfield	14.0
'01 DUKE	Mike Krzyzewski	RONNIE McCOLLUM, Centenary	29.1	CHRIS MARCUS, Western Kentucky	12.1
'02 MARYLAND	Gary Williams	JASON CONLEY, VMI	29.3	JEREMY BISHOP, Quinnipiac	12.0
'03 SYRACUSE	Jim Boeheim	RUBEN DOUGLAS, New Mexico	28.0	BRANDON HUNTER, Ohio	12.6
'04 CONNECTICUT	Jim Calhoun	KEYDREN CLARK, St. Peter's	26.7	PAUL MILLSAP, Louisiana Tech	12.5
'05 NORTH CAROLINA	Roy Williams	KEYDREN CLARK, St. Peter's	25.8	PAUL MILLSAP, Louisiana Tech	12.4
'06 FLORIDA	Billy Donovan	ADAM MORRISON, Gonzaga	28.1	PAUL MILLSAP, Louisiana Tech	13.3
'07 FLORIDA	Billy Donovan	REGGIE WILLIAMS, VMI	28.1	RASHAD JONES-JENNINGS, UALR**	13.1
'08 KANSAS	Bill Self	REGGIE WILLIAMS, VMI	27.8	MICHAEL BEASLEY, Kansas State	12.4
'09 NORTH CAROLINA	Roy Williams	STEPHEN CURRY, Davidson	28.6	BLAKE GRIFFIN, Oklahoma	14.4
'10 DUKE	Mike Krzyzewski	AUBREY COLEMAN, Houston	25.6	ARTSIOM PARAKHOUSKI, Radford	13.4
'11 CONNECTICUT	Jim Calhoun	JIMMER FREDETTE, BYU	28.9	KENNETH FARIED, Morehead State	14.5

* DENOTES YEAR IN WHICH SEASON ENDED **UNIVERSITY OF ARKANSAS–LITTLE ROCK

>> WISH YOU WERE THERE

Illinois 90, Arizona 89 (OT)

MARCH 26, 2005 • ALLSTATE ARENA, ROSEMONT, ILL.
Trailing by 15 points with 3:55 to go in the NCAA regional final, the Illini, led by Luther Head's eight points, outscore the Wildcats 20-5 to force overtime. Down seven in OT with 1:56 left, Hassan Adams scores Arizona's final five points but his three at the buzzer misses high off the backboard.

George Mason 86, UConn 84 (OT) >

MARCH 26, 2006 • VERIZON CENTER, WASHINGTON, D.C.
Playing before a partisan crowd not far from its Fairfax, Va., campus, 11th-seeded George Mason overcomes a nine-point halftime deficit to shock the top-seeded Huskies and advance to its first Final Four. The Patriots get 20 points from 6' 7", 275 pound center Jai Lewis, key buckets from Folarin Campbell *(right)* and survive a missed three-pointer at the buzzer from UConn's Denham Brown to win it.

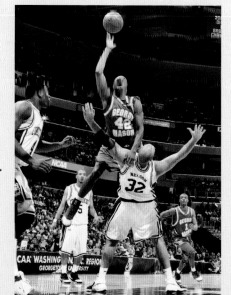

Kansas 75, Memphis 68 (OT)

APRIL 7, 2008 • ALAMODOME, SAN ANTONIO Jayhawks guard Mario Chalmers hits a three-pointer from the top of the arc with 2.1 seconds left in regulation to cap a nine-point comeback and send the title game to overtime. The Tigers' Chris Douglas-Roberts and Derrick Rose hit just one of five free throws in the final 1:15 of regulation to open the door for Kansas's comeback and OT win.

Syracuse 127, UConn 117 (6OT)

MARCH 12, 2009 • MADISON SQUARE GARDEN
Orange guard Eric Devendorf hits a 28-foot jumper for an apparent game-winner at the end of regulation in the Big East tournament quarterfinal, but officials rule it came too late, triggering the game that wouldn't end. The Orange never lead in any of the first five extra sessions and eight players in all foul out. A record 102 points are scored after regulation. The game lasts three hours and 46 minutes, the second-longest Division I game ever.

Duke 61, Butler 59

APRIL 5, 2010 • LUCAS OIL STADIUM, INDIANAPOLIS
For an instant it appears that Butler's Gordon Heyward might make the most dramatic shot in basketball history, but his half-court prayer rattles off the rim as time expires in the title game. Had it gone in, Duke coach Mike Krzyzewski might still be explaining his decision to have center Brian Zoubek intentionally miss his second free throw after making the first.

GAME CHANGER
JOHN CALIPARI
DRIBBLE-DRIVE OFFENSE

Coach Cal adapted his offense from a little-known junior-college coach named Vance Walberg, and it perfectly suits the one-on-one skills of Calipari's talented recruits. In one phase *(left)*, the point guard (1) drives into the middle where he can go for a layup or dish to the post (5) or to an open perimeter player (2, 3 or 4). In the middle diagram, the point dribbles to the elbow and passes to the shooting guard (2) who can take a three-pointer or attack the basket. When a good shot isn't available, cycle and repeat *(right)*.

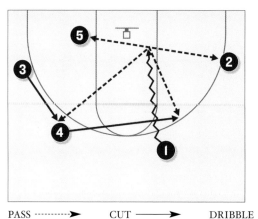 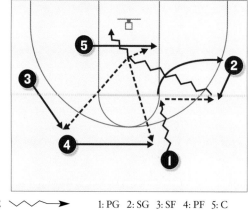 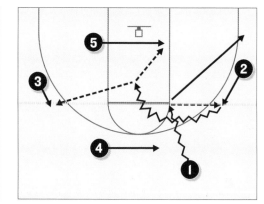

PASS --------> CUT ⟶ DRIBBLE ⌇⟶ 1: PG 2: SG 3: SF 4: PF 5: C

being only a freshman, Anthony led them to a national championship, capped off by a 20-point, 10-rebound performance in the title game against Kansas to earn MVP honors.

THE WOMAN A two-time Naismith Award winner and the key part of two national championship teams, UConn's Maya Moore finished her career in 2011 as the fourth-leading scorer in NCAA women's basketball history. A mark of her versatility is that she's the only Division I women's player with more than 3,000 points, 1,000 rebounds, 500 assists, 300 steals

on Nov. 16, 2008 that did not end until Dec. 30, 2010, 90 straight wins. Similar to UCLA, whose streak was bookended by losses to Notre Dame, the Huskies began their string after a loss to Stanford and ended it against them. The Huskies won by a 33 points average and trailed for just 133 minutes, 58 seconds of a possible 3,600 minutes.

THE CINDERELLA Butler forever changed the landscape of college ball by advancing from the mid-major Horizon League to consecutive NCAA title games in 2010 and '11. Led by coach Brad Stevens, an Indianan in his early 30s, the Bulldogs set an example for small programs that will last for years.

Saying cheese at Wisconsin in 2002.

BASKETBALL BABYLON
A MURDER IN WACO

In the most sordid college basketball story ever, Baylor forward Carlton Dotson *(left)* was convicted and sentenced to 35 years for the murder of teammate Patrick Dennehy in 2003. And when it seemed the story couldn't get any worse, it was learned that Baylor coach Dave Bliss had improperly paid Dennehy's tuition after the forward transferred from New Mexico, then advised his players and staff to lie to investigators and slander Dennehy, saying he'd paid his tuition with money from drug dealing. The NCAA hit the disgraced Bliss with a 10-year show-cause order to keep him from coaching again, while Baylor gave up all nonconference games for a year.

team of the decade.

922 Career wins for Herb Magee at Division II Philadelphia University, the most in NCAA history at any level.

41.9 Three-point field goal attempts per game by VMI in '06-07, a single-season record.

30 Losses in 1999–2000 for Grambling, the only team in major college history to lose 30 in a season.

18.8 Field goal percentage shot by Butler in its 53–41 loss to UConn in the 2011 championship game—the lowest mark in title-game history.

10.8 *Billions* of dollars paid by CBS and Turner Broadcasting for 14 years of NCAA tournament rights, starting in 2011.

2001 | JAMEER NELSON of St. Joseph's took a pass on the defensive efforts of Gonzaga's Ronny Turiaf in a New Year's Eve game in Philly. | *Photograph by* MICHAEL J. LEBRECHT II

2009 | A DISH well served from Syracuse's Jonny Flynn evaded the hungry D of UConn's Kemba Walker (15) and Hasheem Thabeet. | *Photograph by* AL TIELEMANS

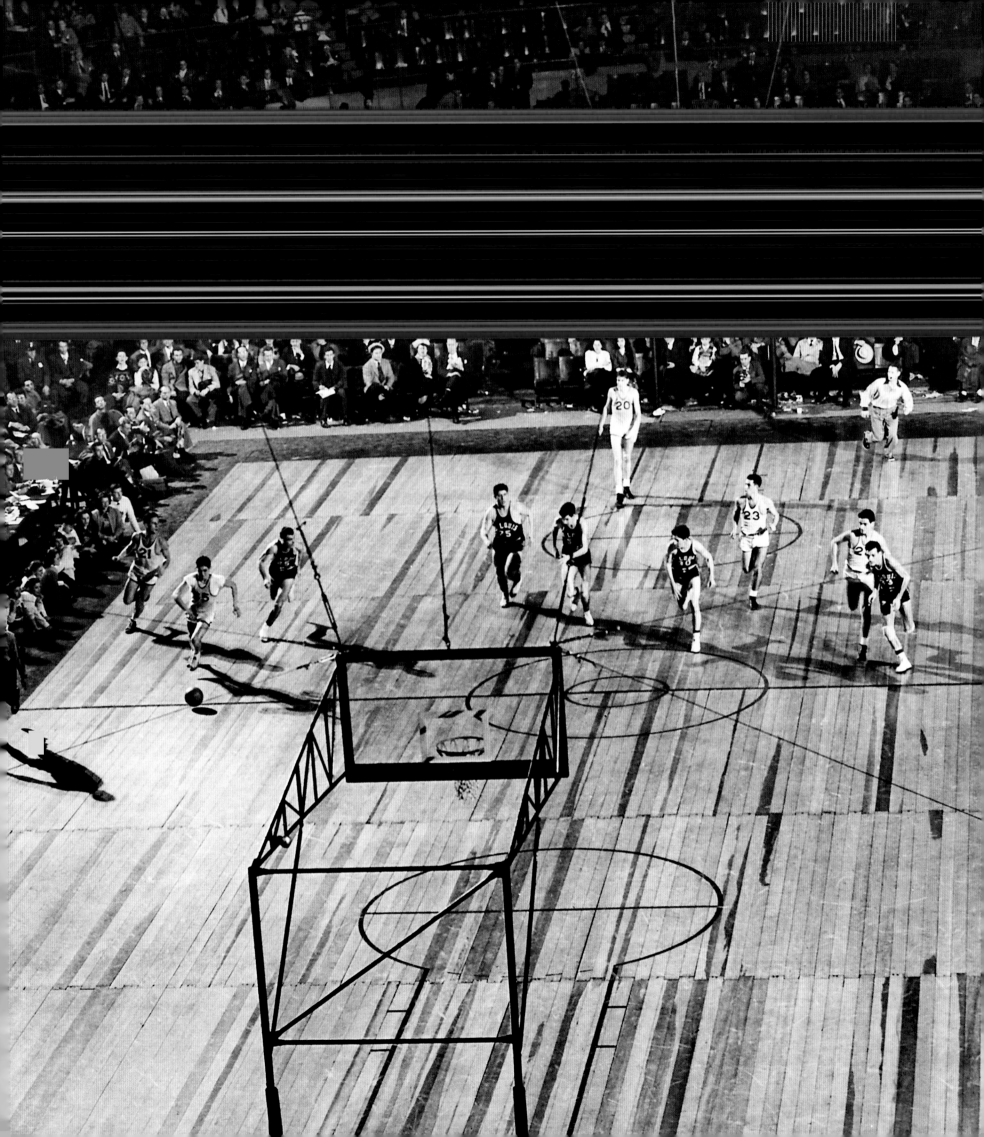

1958 | A KANSAS CHEERLEADER looked up to Wilt Chamberlain and put the lie to his famous quote that "nobody roots for Goliath." | *Photograph by* STAN WAYMAN

1962 | BANDEMONIUM RULED at UCLA's first Final Four, the start of a record 18 appearances by the Bruins and their brassy backers. | *Photograph by* JOHN G. ZIMMERMAN

OUT OF THE DARKNESS

BY GRANT WAHL

A pair of crucial missed free throws by Memphis's Darius Washington went from a moment of infamy to a lesson in humanity. from SI, OCTOBER 15, 2005

LOOK AT HIM. HE'S ALL ALONE. You remember. You saw the replay, over and over, an endless loop on *SportsCenter*. You saw Darius Washington at the free throw line, all zeroes on the clock, his Memphis team down by two to Louisville. You recall the stakes: three free throws to win the game, the Conference USA tournament and a surprise berth in the NCAA field of 65. Three free throws for a slice of Memphis immortality.

He sank the first. "Two to go!" boomed CBS commentator Verne Lundquist.

The 19-year-old freshman, a 72% free throw shooter, turned to the Tigers' bench in Memphis's FedExForum and—get this—winked. It's over, he thought to himself.

He stepped to the line, bounced the ball three times . . . and missed. The vise tightened: OT or bust. "Verne," said Lundquist's partner, Jim Spanarkel, "I would be hard-pressed to tell you right now that you'll see a more pressurized situation this year."

Everyone stood. Tigers coach John Calipari paced the sideline. Angst-ridden Memphis players linked arms on the bench. Washington took a long, deep breath and released the ball.

The last free throw bounced once on the rim. It bounced twice. It bounced off.

Louisville 75, Memphis 74.

The image remains burned in the memories of college basketball fans. Washington wheeled toward the bench, his lower lip quivering, and as he fell to his knees he reached instinctively for his jersey. Years ago his father, also named Darius, had taught his only son a lesson: It's O.K. to cry, but cover your face with your shirt, because the photographers are always there. For three . . . four . . . five seconds he lay facedown in the lane, sobbing, as eerily lonesome a sight as Dustin Hoffman suspended underwater in the pool in *The Graduate*.

Funny thing about images and memory, though. When replays take on lives of their own, it's easy to lose track of what preceded them: in Washington's case, his game-high 23 points. Nor do they tell the story of what came next. You saw the replay, over and over, but you probably didn't see the aftermath. You didn't see a family, a team and a city make sure that Darius Washington wouldn't suffer alone.

Put Washington in a Memphis Grizzlies uniform and he'd probably have earned a spot on the trading block. But something about his visceral reaction, something about college sports, sparked an outpouring of support that spread like a benevolent virus through Memphis and points beyond.

Forrest Goodman was hosting the postgame show on WMC, the Tigers' flagship radio station. His switchboard stayed lit so long that he extended his broadcast. "Grown men were calling, and you could tell they were in tears," he says. "Had Darius missed those free throws and just shrugged, they never would have done that. But you can't fake what he did."

Eli Morris gave the sermon that weekend at Memphis's Hope Presbyterian Church, where he's an associate pastor. "Darius Washington represents our own brokenness right now," he said from the pulpit, "and we need to stand with him and pray for him." The congregation, more than 6,000 strong, broke into applause.

More than 100 letters would pour into the Tigers' basketball office: a note from Temple coach John Chaney, a get-well card from Louisville fans, a letter signed by 32 members of a prayer group, a collage from a four-year-old girl, and enough citations of Romans 8:28 and Jeremiah 29: 11-14 to start a revival meeting.

But one man in particular helped Washington conquer the most excruciating episode of his young life.

Is Darius O.K.? From the moment his son hit the floor, the question kept racing through the head of Darius's father, who was standing with his wife behind the opposing basket. "That's my son out there," he told security officials, and within seconds he was running toward a still-sobbing Darius Jr.

The assistant recreation director of a community center in Winter Park, Fla., the elder Darius says that, at 36, he may be the youngest father of any player in college basketball. "Darius and I kind of grew up together," he explains.

It was his dad who cried with Darius in a vacant room at the arena, who hugged him and said, "You're not in this alone." It was his dad who made Darius watch the replays again and again, to confront his anguish. And it was his dad who took his son for a walk through the Saturday-night crowds on Beale Street a few hours later. "That was a risky move," the father recalls, "but when I did, everybody just mobbed him. *Don't worry about it! We'll get 'em next time!* Nothing negative. We were just letting them know that we're not going to run and hide from this." . . .

AN ANGUISHED Washington covered his face in shame after missing two free throws that would have sent Memphis to the NCAA tournament in 2005.

1976 | PIONEERING COACH Margaret Wade made Delta State the Cadillac of early women's programs, winning three straight national championships in the '70s. | *Photograph by* JAMES DRAKE

1983 | LEPRECHAUN-SIZED COACH Lou Carnesecca celebrated with Chris Mullin (20) and Kevin Williams after St. John's won its first Big East tournament. | *Photograph by* ANDY HAYT

2008 | MICHAEL BEASLEY was hailed as a conquering hero as Kansas State ended 24 years of home-court futility against Kansas with an 84–75 win. | *Photograph by* DAVID E. KLUTHO

THE PERFECT GAME

BY TIM LAYDEN

Villanova was an eighth seed in the 1985 NCAA tournament—the last to be played without a shot clock—and it shocked top-ranked Georgetown and the world to win the national championship. To this day the Wildcats are still the lowest seed ever to win it all.
—from SI, MARCH 29, 2004

THIS GAME NEVER LETS GO. Nineteen years are gone now since Villanova senior forward Dwayne McClain stumbled to his knees and elbows on the floor of Rupp Arena, then cradled the last precious inbounds pass in his right arm and shot his left fist skyward as time expired. Nineteen years have passed since Villanova's 66–64 victory over Georgetown on an April Fools' night thrust the Wildcats into underdog lore as a team that played the perfect game on the grandest stage against the toughest foe. Coaches everywhere were instantly and forever given license to dream aloud, inspiring their teams to do the impossible.

The memory of that game moves many of the '85 players to the edge of tears. "Just talking about it, right now, the hair is standing up on the back of my neck," says Wyatt Maker, a reserve sophomore center, who sat on the bench clutching the hand of junior teammate Chuck Everson, twin seven-footers willing shots into the basket like schoolgirl cheerleaders.

Others hold more than just memories. Harold Jensen, the sophomore head case recruited from Trumbull (Conn.) High to shoot from the outside, conquered his self-doubt only during the tournament run and made the most important shot in Villanova history, an 18-foot jumper that gave the Wildcats a 55–54 lead with 2:37 to play in the title game. Four years later, at the age of 24, Jensen and a partner started Showtime Enterprises, a marketing company that now employs 125 people in six offices. "That season, that tournament was a turning point in my life beyond the sport," says Jensen. "It taught me to believe in myself, and I've taken that through my whole life."

At 5 a.m. the day before the final, the Villanova coaching staff met in coach Rollie Massimino's hotel room and plotted a strategy. Earlier in the season, coach John Thompson's Hoyas had beaten Villanova 52–50 in overtime at the Spectrum and 57–50 in Landover, Md. "Coach Thompson wasn't going to change much for us, we knew that," says Mitch Buonaguro, the assistant coach who was responsible for the championship game scouting report. "So we stuck with what we did, and added a couple of little wrinkles." The Wildcats would play their array of zone defenses and, on Georgetown's first pass would often switch to a matchup or man-to-man. "The goal," says Steve Lappas, another assistant, "was to make Georgetown run a zone offense while we were playing man-to-man, and they wouldn't realize it."

"Offensively," says Massimino, "we just tweaked a few things to make sure we got the ball to Eddie Pinckney," the Wildcats 6' 9½" center, who was giving up 2½ inches and 35 pounds to the Hoyas' All-America center, Patrick Ewing. "He loved to play against Patrick," Massimino says. One other thing they would do: Put the ball in point guard Gary McLain's hands and let him beat Georgetown's swarming, 94-foot defense with his skills, his head and his heart. It was a daunting assignment and would require the game of his life.

The game that unfolded the next night was a work of art. It started when Pinckney took the ball directly at Ewing on an early possession and dealt a soft pass to forward Harold Pressley, who willed in a wild reverse layup. McClain dunked on the next Villanova possession. Before the night was finished Villanova would make 22 of 28 field goal attempts, a mind-boggling 78.6%, including nine of 10 in the second half. McLain was flawless and cocksure with the ball against pressure, Jensen shot 5 for 5, and Pinckney, playing with the flu, had 16 points and six rebounds to Ewing's 14 and five.

A key point came with six minutes to play. The Wildcats had held a 53–48 advantage, but Georgetown ran off six straight points to take the lead, forced a Villanova turnover and went into a four corners in an attempt to coax Villanova into a man-to-man defense. The stall lasted less than half a minute before the Hoyas turned the ball over.

Villanova then held the ball for 62 seconds until Jensen bravely drilled the wide-open jump shot from the right side with 2:37 left. The Wildcats did not trail again. When they returned to their hotel, so many fans awaited that the players couldn't get off the bus. "We were like the Beatles," says Pinckney.

Unlike all of his players, Massimino has never watched the entire championship game tape. A little of the first half, a little of the second, but never the whole game and never the finish. "You know why?" he asks, leaning forward. There is a pause, and Massimino's eyes dance like old. "I'm afraid we'll lose." . . .

HE GAVE up 2½ inches and 35 pounds to Ewing, but Pinckney (54) outscored the Hoyas center to lead the Wildcats to perhaps the greatest tournament upset ever.

1954 | LEAPING LA SALLE and Duquesne players filled the air in a Dukes win at Madison Square Garden's Holiday Festival in Manhattan (N.Y.). | *Photograph by* RICHARD MEEK

2011 | THE JUMPING is higher and the footwear better, but the game looked essentially the same when Kansas met Kansas State in Manhattan (Kans.). | *Photograph by* GREG NELSON

2002 | GLOOMY GATORS LaDarius Halton (left) and Orien Greene moped in the Georgia Dome locker room after Florida's quarterfinal exit from the SEC tournament. | *Photograph by* BILL FRAKES

2011 | CONFETTI STREAMED and UConn reigned after the Huskies beat Butler in Houston for their third national championship in 13 years. | *Photograph by* RICH CLARKSON

Acknowledgments

MANY THANKS MUST FIRST GO TO ALL THE fine writers and photographers who have covered college basketball since SPORTS ILLUSTRATED's inception in 1954, with a special nod to Rich Clarkson, whose archives were particularly invaluable. His photographs here run from Dean Smith at Kansas in 1951—shot when Clarkson himself was a student at the school—to UConn's celebration of its NCAA title in 2011, with scores of wonderful images in between. A debt is also owed to past hoops editors Larry Keith, Peter Carry, Dick Friedman and Aimee Crawford for their help in selecting the stories excerpted within.

For their invaluable contributions our gratitude also goes to Steve Fine, Porter Binks, Karen Carpenter, Prem Kalliat, Joe Felice and George Amores in the SI photo and picture syndication departments, and to Geoff Michaud, Dan Larkin, Bob Thompson and the rest of the SI Imaging group. Thanks also to Joy Birdsong and Susan Szeliga in the SI Library, and to the staff at the Naismith Memorial Basketball Hall of Fame. And a very special thank you to Time Inc. Sports Group editor Terry McDonell for his support and encouragement. And finally, to all the players and coaches who have made the game such a joy to explore in these pages, thanks for doing what you did.

1969 | LEW ALCINDOR'S
LOW-TOP CONVERSE

Cover images colorized by SI Imaging.

COVER CREDITS: FRONT (Top to bottom, from left): John W. McDonough, Rich Clarkson (2), Bill Frakes; Rich Clarkson (2), Damian Strohmeyer, Andy Hayt; John Biever, Rich Clarkson, Damian Strohmeyer, Rich Clarkson; NCAA Photos, Heinz Kluetmeier, Bill Frakes (2); George Gojkovich/Getty Images, Rich Clarkson/Rich Clarkson & Associates, Heinz Kluetmeier, Manny Millan; Rich Clarkson, Tony Tomsic, Lou Capozzola, John D. Hanlon; Rich Clarkson (2), John Iacono, Heinz Kluetmeier. BACK (Top to bottom, from left): Bill Feig/AP, Cliff Schiappa/AP, Art Shay, Rich Clarkson/Rich Clarkson & Associates; Bettmann/Corbis, Richard Phillips, Anthony Neste, John W. McDonough; Rich Clarkson, Richard Mackson, Hugh Morton, John D. Hanlon; Rich Clarkson/Rich Clarkson & Associates, Bettmann/Corbis, Manny Millan, John Iacono; AP, Nelson Chenault/US Presswire, Rich Clarkson, ODU Athletic Department; John Biever (2), Manny Millan, Greg Nelson; Long Photography, Elsa/Getty Images, Bettmann/Corbis, Temple Sports Information. FRONT FLAP (Top to bottom, from left): Doug Hoke, Bruce Roberts, Manny Millan, Bill Frakes; James Drake, Fred Kaplan, Al Tielemans, John Iacono. BACK FLAP (Top to bottom, from left): Todd J. Van Emst/Opelika-Auburn News/ AP; Stanford University/NCAA Photos, James Drake; Heinz Kluetmeier, NCAA Photos, John Biever, Robert Beck. SPINE (Top to bottom): Rich Clarkson, Manny Millan, Jim Gund, John W. McDonough.

TABLE OF CONTENTS (Top to bottom, from left): Manny Millan, Rich Clarkson, John Iacono, John Biever; Rich Clarkson, John Biever, Manny Millan; Heinz Kluetmeier, Andy Hayt, Bill Frakes; Mark Kauffman, John W. McDonough, John Biever, James Drake.

PICTURES: Icon SMI: 22; Time Life Pictures/Getty Images: 28, 148, 239, 241; AP: 54; Reuters: 113; The Detroit News: 117; Wireimage.com: 140, 218; Getty Images: 151, 214; Rich Clarkson & Associates: 183, 195;

The Washington Post: 184; The Jonesboro Sun: 185; US Presswire: 190-191; 196-197; Corbis Outline: 217; The Oklahoman/AP: 228; Aurora Photos: 232; IDeuce3 Photography: 236.

MOVIE POSTERS (From top, left to right): The Everett Collection (2), Buena Vista Pictures/The Everett Collection (2), Paramount Pictures, The Everett Collection (2).

HARDWOOD TO DIAMONDS (From top, left to right): Mark Rucker/ Transcendental Graphics/Getty Images, Courtesy of Creighton Athletics, Ohio State Department of Athletics, Heinz Kluetmeier, Peter Read Miller, Beverly Schaefer.

COLLEGE OF COACHES: Jackson: UND Athletics, John W. McDonough; Nelson: Iowa Sports Information, John W. McDonough; Wilkens: Providence College Athletics, John W. McDonough; Sloan: Rich Clarkson, John W. McDonough; Riley: Rich Clarkson, David Bergman; Brown: North Carolina/Collegiate Images/Getty Images, Bill Frakes; Karl: Rich Clarkson, John W. McDonough.

REFEREES (From top, left to right): Bob Rosato, Karl DeBlaker/AP, Porter Binks, Greg Nelson, David E. Klutho (2).

PRE-1950s: Essay (from top): Frank Scherschel/Time Life Pictures/Getty Images, University of Oregon; Wish You Were There: Hugh Morton; Game Changer: Bettmann/Corbis; Time Capsule: Special Collections/NCSU Libraries; Basketball Babylon: Charles Knoblock/AP; TV: H. Armstrong Roberts/ClassicStock/Corbis (set), NCAA Photos.

1950s: Essay: KM Archive/Getty Images; Wish You Were There: Marvin E. Newman; Game Changer: John D. Hanlon; Time Capsule: Marvin E. Newman; Basketball Babylon: AP; TV: SSPL/Getty Images (set), Richard Meek.

1960s: Essay: Elliott Landy/Redferns/Getty Images; Wish You Were There: Rich Clarkson; Game Changer: Stephen Green-Armytage; Time Capsule: James Drake; Basketball Babylon: Saxon/AP; TV: Lawrence Manning/Corbis (set), Harvey Eugene Smith/AP.

1970s: Essay: Sunset Boulevard/Corbis; Wish You Were There: Rich Clarkson; Game Changer: Rich Clarkson; Time Capsule: Rich Clarkson; Basketball Babylon: Clemson/Collegiate Images/Getty Images; TV: Shutterstock (set), James Drake.

1980s: Essay: Regis Bossu/Sygma/Corbis; Wish You Were There: Rich Clarkson; Game Changer: Rich Clarkson; Time Capsule: John W. McDonough; Basketball Babylon: NOPD Records; TV: Shutterstock (set), John W. McDonough.

1990s: Essay: Vince Bucci/Pool/AP; Wish You Were There: Damian Strohmeyer; Game Changer: Peter Gregoire; Time Capsule: Rich Clarkson/ NCAA Photos; Basketball Babylon: John Biever; TV: Erick W. Rasco (set), Rich Clarkson/NCAA Photos.

2000s: Essay: Paul Sakuma/AP; Wish You Were There: John Biever; Game Changer: Bob Rosato; Time Capsule: David Stluka/Icon SMI; Basketball Babylon: Ron Aydelotte/Waco Tribune Herald; TV: Bill Frakes.

TIME HOME ENTERTAINMENT: Richard Fraiman, PUBLISHER; Steven Sandonato, GENERAL MANAGER; Carol Pittard, EXECUTIVE DIRECTOR, MARKETING SERVICES; Tom Mifsud, EXECUTIVE DIRECTOR, RETAIL & SPECIAL SALES; Peter Harper, EXECUTIVE DIRECTOR, NEW PRODUCT DEVELOPMENT; Laura Adam, DIRECTOR, BOOKAZINE DEVELOPMENT & MARKETING; Joy Butts, PUBLISHING DIRECTOR; Helen Wan, ASSISTANT GENERAL COUNSEL; Anne-Michelle Gallero, DESIGN & PREPRESS MANAGER; Susan Chodakiewicz, BOOK PRODUCTION MANAGER; Allison Parker, BRAND MANAGER; Alex Voznesenskiy, ASSOCIATE PREPRESS MANAGER

DAVID N. BERKWITZ COURTESY OF NAISMITH MEMORIAL BASKETBALL HALL OF FAME